INTRODUCTION

Angela Mao
THE DEADLY CHINA DOLL
By Rick Baker

I love putting these specials together, showcasing the true icons of Hong Kong Cinema. We recently did a special on Jackie Chan with Brett Ratner, and as I compile this issue we are working on "The Sammo Hung Special" it's all go! Back in 1973, martial arts performer Angela Mao Ying was as famous as Bruce Lee in the United States. Her film Hapkido (known as Lady Kung Fu there) even knocked Lee's Enter the Dragon, in which she played Lee's sister, off the top of the US box-office charts for a week. She managed her career well and featured in more than 40 films between 1968 and 1992. Her major films include Hapkido, Lady Whirlwind (bizarrely retitled with the erotic title Deep Thrust in the US) and When Taekwondo Strikes Mao also had a role in King Hu's wuxia film The Fate of Lee Khan.

女活殺拳

During this time, she built up strong working relationships with Hong Kong martial arts actor Sammo Hung, who often choreographed her films and appeared in supporting roles; with Carter Wong, with whom she formed an on-screen partnership; and with director Huang Feng, with whom she later formed a production company. People of my age had their first glimpse of Angela when they took their seat in the cinema back in 1974 to watch "Enter the Dragon" as a small whirlwind enters the screen! A miniature deadly China doll if you will cutting a very striking presence on the screen

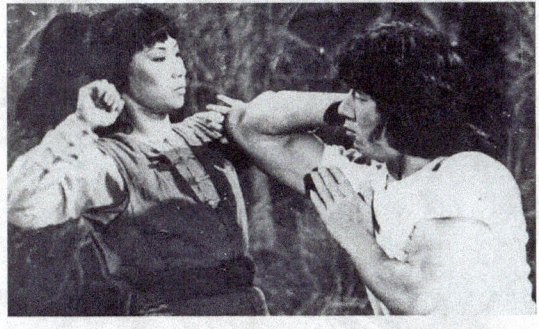

You set your eyes on her for the first time playing Su Lin (Bruce lee's sister in the movie) in a flashback being pursued by O'Harra and his men. Despite her limited screen time, her presence had you transfixed to her fighting skills; she has a simultaneous expression of anger and restraint as she goes into battle proving she is a force to be reckoned with if you go too far. It was said in an interview by one of her sons that when they saw that look when growing up, they knew they were in trouble. I was hooked from the first moment she entered my movie going world, seeking out any information

and watching any films that managed to reach the UK cinemas and pursuing Hong Kong Movies stars was to become a large part of my life, and still is to this day! I could say so much more, but I have been lucky that thank you to Frank Djeng (鄭曉霖) and Simon Pritchard worked together to get an exclusive interview with Ms Mao and along the way got many ethers to pay their respects for this special issue Dedicated to her career. So I am leaving those pages in this special hardback to them as a thank you for their time in helping make this special edition possible.

So Thank you everyone and a special thank you to Angela who has such an influential part of my life.

THE MISSION TO THE QUEEN OF KUNG FU

By Simon Pritchard

A long time ago in a village in Wiltshire far far away… before internet shopping caught on and digital media was a thing of science-fiction; the UK high street was at its peak with shops such as HMV, Tower Records, Virgin Megastore, MVC, Our Price, Woolworths, second-hand shops plus many more.

With VHS still readily available and DVDs just coming out, the stores were stocked full of films from Hollywood blockbusters to the most obscure and cult movies. The popularity of films at this time was also due to when Andreas Whittam Smith was appointed the President of the British Board of Film Classification (BBFC). Andreas instigated the liberalisation of film and video censorship. This paved the way for so many old films being re-released, international distributors licensing their films for the first time in the UK market which included Eastern Asian cinema and Kung Fu…

At this time, my friend Mark Chant and I were spending what little money we had on the latest J-Horror, Wuxia, and 'new' old school kung fu films. After seeing "18 Bronzemen" and several Sammo Hung films, I got a copy of Hapkido and thought "Sammo, Carter, what could go wrong!?" By the time the first restaurant fight had finished I knew I had found my favourite martial artist: Angela Mao.

Fast forward about quarter of a century and writing for Eastern Heroes; I said to Ricky Baker that my goal is to interview Angela Mao. Rick said, "If you do, of course I'll print it". With no clue how to achieve this and a lot of willingness & determination, with a little bit of 'healthy' stubbornness mixed in, the mission begun….

After about a year of searching the internet, social media, and other paths that lead nowhere, I emailed Nan Bei Ho and talked with George King, Angela's youngest son, who agreed in principle and I finally had a chance.

I wrote a lot of questions to start with, a little over thirty. YouTuber Johnny "Fanatical Dragon" Burnett and Rick provided feedback and advice, so I revised my questions and cut them down. Johnny's wife, Zhijun Liu, translated the questions and we were ready to go. I sent the questions to George.

A few weeks had gone and I tried to get back in touch but to no avail. I thought the time may have passed. We were so close but so far….

One evening Rick called and said there is a guy called Frank Djeng who has asked if anyone has any questions for Angela as he was meeting her in the next couple of days. At this point I had to sit down and revaluate what I was doing and what I was actually trying to achieve. I realised I am going to need help to do this and the goal is bigger than one man's mission.

I reached out to Frank and explained the situation and thankfully Frank was more than happy to help. Frank and his crew had limited time with filming for the extras for the up-and-coming Eureka Entertainment special edition Blu-rays of Hapkido and Lady Whirlwind. Frank suggested, due to time, that he mix my questions in with his to ensure they were all asked. I agreed.

Working together it just snowballed from there. Not only interviewing Angela, Frank has also interviewed Thomas King, Angela's eldest son. Thomas has spoken about the move to New York, how the family survived, building up a reputation within the community for authentic Taiwanese cooking, Angela's view on fame and more. To add further depth to the story we have spoken with Angela's friends, customers and fans; to bring you currently the most in-depth interview and review of "The Original Queen of Martial Arts Cinema", Angela Mao.

BROKEN OATH
(A Synopsis)

In the waning years of the Ming Dynasty, China is threatened by the ambitious Manchus. Some high officials, like Tsou, become traitors. General Liu is dismissed for his knowledge of Tsou's treason. Tsou further sends his men to kill the general. The general's wife is banished to an island prison for wounding one of the assassins.

Intent on revenge, the general's wife gets herself pregnant in the prison. Before she dies during birth labour, she writes down the whole story and orders the unborn child to kill Tsou and his assassins. The child is a girl, Elaine.

Elaine is now 20 and a great martial artist. When she learns of her own history, she wastes no time in going after her enemies.

The first assassin killed by Elaine is Hou who tried to rape her mother. But she begins to find it more difficult as Tsou's treason has been exposed and he is hiding.

Elaine still manages to kill another assassin who runs a brothel as a front. But she is herself wounded. She is saved by Wen, the only good man among Tsou's killers.

Meanwhile, Tsou's men are engaged in fights with government agents who come to Elaine's help. After one unsuccessful attempt, Elaine finally comes face to face with Tsou.

監製 鄒文懷
導演 鄭昌和

「破戒」

明末清初,一艘裝着女囚犯的官船駛向狼牙島,船上的女囚犯中,有前總兵劉大雄的妻子綺梅(何㼆)。

船抵狼牙島,綺梅被配到千手娘(王萊)的牢裡,當日晚上,作起惡夢,回憶起往事來。

劉大雄(闌山)因獲悉陰謀叛國的元兇仇魁(張佩山)而被陷害,罷官還故里時,途中被仇魁的四大心腹趙才(陳惠敏)郝式(趙雄)等襲擊,劉大雄被殺,妻子綺梅,被郝式帶走,企圖強姦,綺梅以頭簪將其刺瞎,因而被抓到官裡去,被判終身流放狼牙島,綺梅矢志報仇,於是跟典獄,醫生等亂交,終於懷孕了。十月懷胎,但却難產,為自己的遭遇和冤情,身世等,告知千手娘,待孩子長大後,報此血仇。

轉眼廿餘年,綺梅女兒潔蓮(茅瑛)長得風韻絕代,且練成華山劍及佛門拳法,潔蓮藝成下山,往找乾殺千手娘,獲知自己身世,決心報仇。

飛天鼠(夏雨)對潔蓮像親哥一般的照顧,協助她取了郝式的性命。

另一方面,仇魁陰謀叛國的行爲,而有所聞。即派出密使,仇魁查知另一仇人賣齊在開枝院,乃假作在郝式的殯禮中,將仇魁的爪牙逮捕。

潔蓮查知另一仇人賣齊在開枝院,乃假作賣身混進虎穴,亦報了仇。不過潔蓮自己中了劇毒,幸得本性善良之仇人文允爲他解毒,又以內功救她的命。

另一仇人趙才,也經常在潔蓮危難時出現相救。不過,趙才只不過利用潔蓮報仇心理,協助她除去文允,獨獲仇魁的歡心。潔蓮獲悉後,立即追尋到仇魁的鎮南府去。

趙才與朝廷密使陳邦(梁小龍)楊威(郭振獻)大打出手,先殺楊威,再殺陳邦。陳邦假死得免。此時,潔蓮恰巧潛進仇魁卧室,刺死假仇魁。潔蓮發現仇魁末死,乃會同密使,找着賣國賊仇魁及其殺手,潔蓮殺了仇魁,報了親仇。

FRANK DJENG
INTERVIEW WITH ANGELA MAO

FD: Before we start the interview, can you please introduce yourself.

AM: Hi, my name is Angela Mao, since its 2022 and has only been one month after the year of the tiger, I wish everyone good health and happiness forever.

FD: Can you speak a bit about your childhood, specifically about ballet and the Beijing Opera?

AM: I was born in Taiwan. When I was six, I entered Taiwan's 北投復興戲劇學校 (Beitou Fuxing Opera School) I was trained in Dao Madan (a Chinese opera female character versed in shadowboxing, swordplay etc.)

FD: How many years did you train?

AM: For us it was eight years. It was very tough. Chinese Opera is always tough.

FD: Who were some of your fellow pupils, was there any notable ones?

AM: There was a lot of them. When I was in JiaHe (Golden Harvest), there was Zhang Yi, Tian Jun (James Tien). Shao Shi (Shaw Brothers) had Qin Xiang Lin (Charlie Chin), Tianyi (Tien Ni) Jialing (Jia Ling), and these were all in the same year.

FD: How did you get to know director Huang Feng, and how did you get involved when he wanted to make "The Angry River" (Gui Nu Chuan)?

AM: There was an author named Zhu-Ge Qing Yun. He was my Godfather, and we were very close. He was a good friend with director Huang Feng and he invited the director to watch my opera show. Back then I was in Liang Qing Jun. The director said I could do it that was back when we started Kung Fu (Wuxia) films, that was how I came to know the director.

FD: Your first movie was "The Angry River". Could you talk a bit about your memories on this movie?

AM: Well of course opera and movies were very different. Opera is more about the stage and movies are closer to daily life. As we have trained eight years, nearly ten years in opera, every time we stepped on stage there was this opera style showcase and introduction. The director had to slowly change these habits. When it came to movies, one big difference from opera was that we never needed to go to

鐵掌旋風腿

這是發生於民初的故事。巾幗英雄田麗君，為了姐姐的被遺棄而死，到一個小鎮上找薄倖郎凌世豪洩憤。但抵達小鎮，大鬧一場之後，却聽到了一個使她失望的消息：凌世豪因為不甘為當地惡勢力刁大娘賣命，已為刁大娘的手下所殺。

可是後來她在另一個少女王霜霜身上，找到線索，發現凌世豪並沒有死，他在三年前被刁大娘手下鄧石平處死時，並未斷氣，給王霜霜救活，三年來不斷練功，正準備找刁大娘報仇雪恨。於是，劇情急轉直下，恩恩怨怨的關係，也就錯綜複雜起來。一方面是田麗君糾纏着凌世豪決鬥，另方面刁大娘這邊，勢力相當雄厚，除了擁有一個空手道九段高手東谷太郎及一個柔道况兼手下人多勢衆，凌世豪怎麼說也不是刁大娘的敵手。

當凌世豪和王霜霜悄然擺脫了田麗君的糾纏，到達小鎮，雖然手刃三年前奉命鎗，並且身受埋處死。

田麗君隨欲讓他養好傷王霜霜，麗君王霜霜救了凌原來凌世上救了一位恩太極拳法全部凌世豪終楚楚可憐，甚刁大娘報仇世豪練戚，終於碰但是事的終結後關頭及楚楚可豪生命的

導演茅吳京洪金

嘉聯出品　GH　嘉禾發行

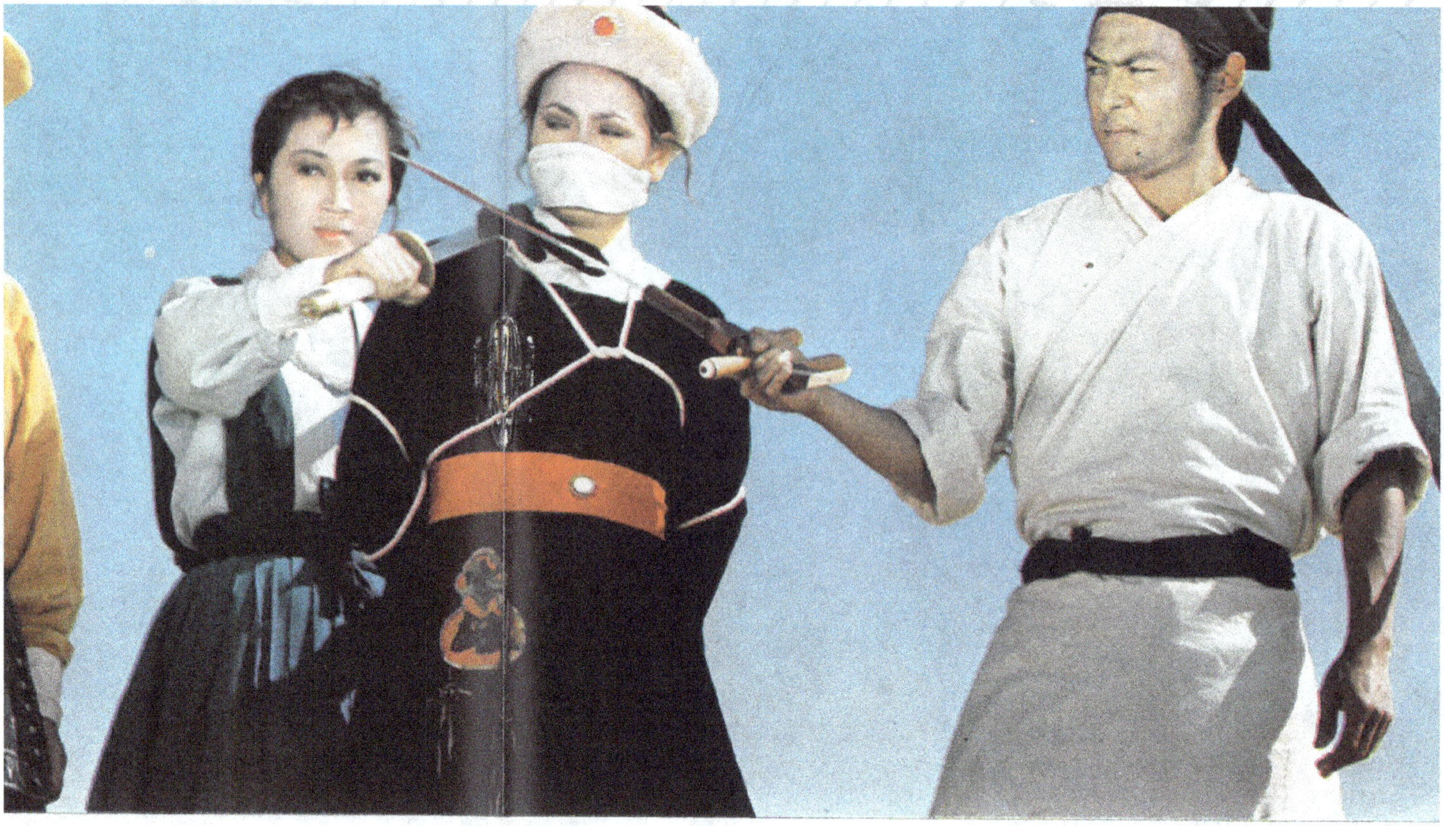

之風波 片中兩幕　緊張高潮

上：萬人迷挾持李婉兒向李察罕要脅放人。
下：黑牡丹，水蜜桃，夜來香擒拿劫賊。

ALTERNATIVE COVER IMAGE

extremely hot or extremely cold places to work. We never needed to wear winter clothes in the summer or summer clothes in the winter. This was quite tough to deal with. The rest was easier to handle, and it just took time and practice.

FD: Director Huang Feng could be called a hero. He was a pioneer. It could be said that he started the business of kung fu movie. As his student what was most memorable in your collaboration with him?

AM: How did you say? He was very careful. Golden Harvest was a new company; he was the director, so he had to find these people. It was the time that kung fu movies were at its peak in terms of popularity. The people had to have backgrounds from ballet, Chinese Opera, or sports. When I started, for me, he was a really good teacher. I was alone in Hong Kong, and he had a family, so he and his wife and daughter all treated me really well. He took care of everything for me when I was in Hong Kong.

FD: Back then when Raymond Chow left Shaw Brothers Pictures International Limited and started his company, you were his first star, before Bruce Lee. How big of an impact did Chow play on your movie career?

AM: We all watched Shaw Brothers movies when we grew up. So, when director Huang Feng came to Taiwan to find me, we all had a feeling that: "wow, I am going to be a celebrity!" Back then the company was in Hong Kong. There were Miao Ke Xiu (Nora Miao), Yiyi and me. Yiyi and I were the first from Taiwan. Mr. Chow took care of us as youngsters. They have seen too many big stars.

FD: People say the biggest difference between Shaw Brothers and Golden Harvest was that Raymond Chow allowed his directors to be free. The feel of Golden Harvest movies was seen to be not as factory (structured) as the Shaw Brothers. Do you agree that being in Golden Harvest was freer and more creative?

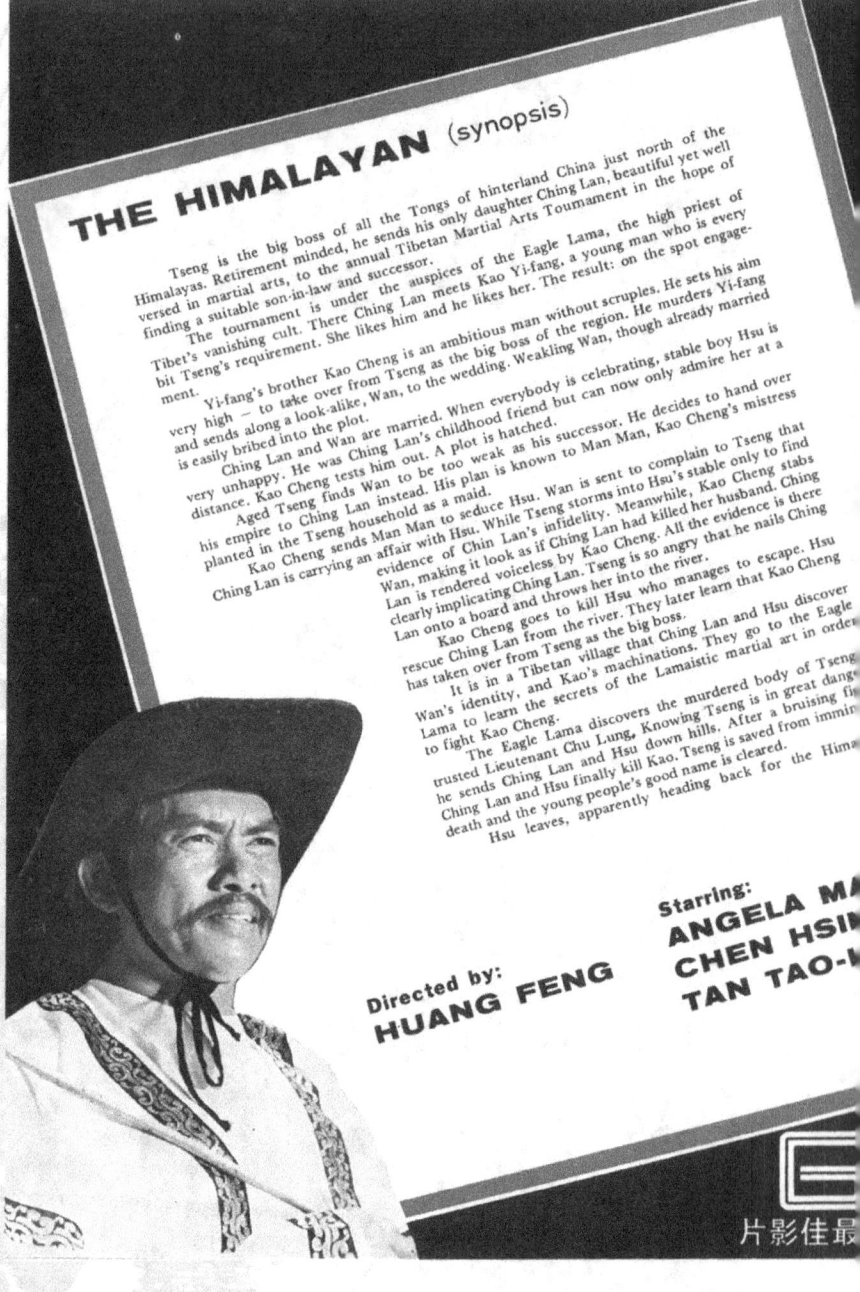

AM: Yes, back then I was new to the movie circle. I entered for only a few months. It was not until I was in "Lady Kung Fu" which was two years after I entered movies that I knew, from a businessman's perspective, that he has to make money. He based the movies on the preference of the audience, so he had to make films like that. More culture heavy and artistic movies (Wen Yi Pian) were not as popular. So, what Golden Harvest had produced was mainly if not all kung fu movies.

FD: Was there a feeling that Golden Harvest was competing with Shaw Brothers, Shaw Brothers were our enemies and we had to make better movies than Shaw Brothers?

AM: I did not have this mentality. As an actor, when we receive the script, we must understand this character and every other role in the movie. We need to understand all of these.

FD: At the time, you made some movies with director Luo Wei, what do you think is the biggest difference between Luo Wei and Huang Feng and what is the biggest difference in their movies?

AM: I filmed "Back Alley Princess" with Luo Wei. I did not play a big role in the movies. Different directors use different camera angles. They also had different styles.

FD: What were the different styles?

AM: They were the senior ones in the industry. No matter how good we were with movies, we didn't have the right to comment.

FD: You were assigned to be the female protagonist; did he face any troubles? Did anyone say "How can a woman be the lead protagonist?"

AM: Oh, no, no, no. There was never this thought. To be honest, at the start it was Shaw Brothers with Cheng Pei Pei in "Come Drink With Me" that brought up the popularity. Golden Harvest popularised that in films about early Chinese Republic. When Bruce Lee came on the scene, it was all kung fu movies in the early Chinese Republic*. But Mr. Chow did not have these thoughts deliberately.

(*Early Chinese Republic usually means the period just after the Chinese revolution that overthrew the Qing dynasty in 1911)

FD: Some audiences say that Golden Harvest was a hero and pioneer in the feminist movement.

AM: No, no, no, no.

FD: What did you feel about this very forward-looking system in Golden Harvest.

AM: I don't think I should be called a hero. I am just thankful for everyone, friends and movie fans for all the praises. I'm very thankful.

FD: When Sammo Hung (Hung Kam Bo), Hang Ying Jie and others were fight choreographers, did they just design the moves or did they also get involved in filming and performing?

AM They also were involved in performing the moves. They had another role in the movie that they were the fight choreographer as well because they were trained in Chinese opera and also in martial arts. Han Ying Jie was a guru. He was very experienced. To be honest, Sammo Hung was also a senior to me. He entered the Hong Kong movie business much earlier than I did.

FD: You also worked with King Hu (Hu Jin Quan). What did you think made Hu Jin Quan one level above all the other kung fu movie directors at the time?

AM Yes, it was because of "Come Drink with Me." He made this movie take off. This level of Kung Fu Movies was popular for a good ten to twenty years. Which made him the best of the best when it came to directors.

FD: Was any of this because he was very familiar to literature?

AM: Might be so. His style was that each day he had a little booklet about the scenes he would do on the day. Square by square, shot by shot with the spots of every character written down and when and where the effects are coming. This makes his production speed very fast.

FD: But you only filmed one movie with director Hu?

AM: Yes, but I knew him for a very long time. I knew him since I was in Taiwan.

FD: When you met Bruce Lee in Golden Harvest, did you think he would become as big of a star that he ended up being?

AM: Oh, when Bruce Lee asked me to film "Enter the Dragon", I was filming "Lady Kung Fu". When "The Big Boss" came out, we watched

吳家驤飾都魯哈赤。　韓英傑飾沙雲山。

苗天飾演曹玉昆。

孫嵐飾沈天松。　魏平澳飾文獸齊。

茅瑛飾演黑牡丹。

白鷹飾演王士誠。

王琛（右）飾老寶商人，吳明才飾小順子。

胡錦飾演水蜜桃。

迎春閣之風波 ·本事·

李察罕在迎春閣內盤問萬人迷等各人。

KING HU PRODUCES HIS OWN FILM

A new film production directed ably by King Hu, and starred by tip-top movie personalities such as Li Li Hua, Hsu Feng, Mao Ying, Chao Hung, Pai Ying, Hu Chun, Helen Ma, Tien Feng and Shang Kuan Yen-er, depicts how the Han heroes tried hard to fight against Yen's force. The plot is specially designed to attrat the utmost attention of the spectators, and provides nice enterainment and effect.

元朝末年，暴政苛捐，民不聊生，不甘受異族統治之有志之士，紛紛起自草莽，展開反元復漢工作，其中之最著者，首推朱元璋。

李察罕乃元室宗族，官河南王之謀客，善武功，其妹婉兒為其得力助手，婉兒得信謂朱元璋部下內奸沈天松，欲獻朱氏之佈兵圖，故李察罕及婉兒帶領侍衛曹玉昆等齊赴京西，此曹玉昆者，明為元官，實為多謀客。

萬人迷者乃女中豪傑也，機智百出，得信後，即利用當地鎮台都魯哈赤為薛山，召來舊友小辣椒—藝名黑牡丹，水蜜桃—一路剷小黑出身，夜來香—騙子出身，扒手出身四女來迎春閣內增設賭館，以吸引徒生意，實則為掩護身侍，明為招徠生意，實則為掩護身侍。

王士誠，沙雲山來迎春閣，旋為萬人迷認做表兒，留在迎春閣帳房，沙雲山亦以王士誠跟班身閣，反元志士王士誠，沙雲山亦以王士誠跟班身閣，反元志士

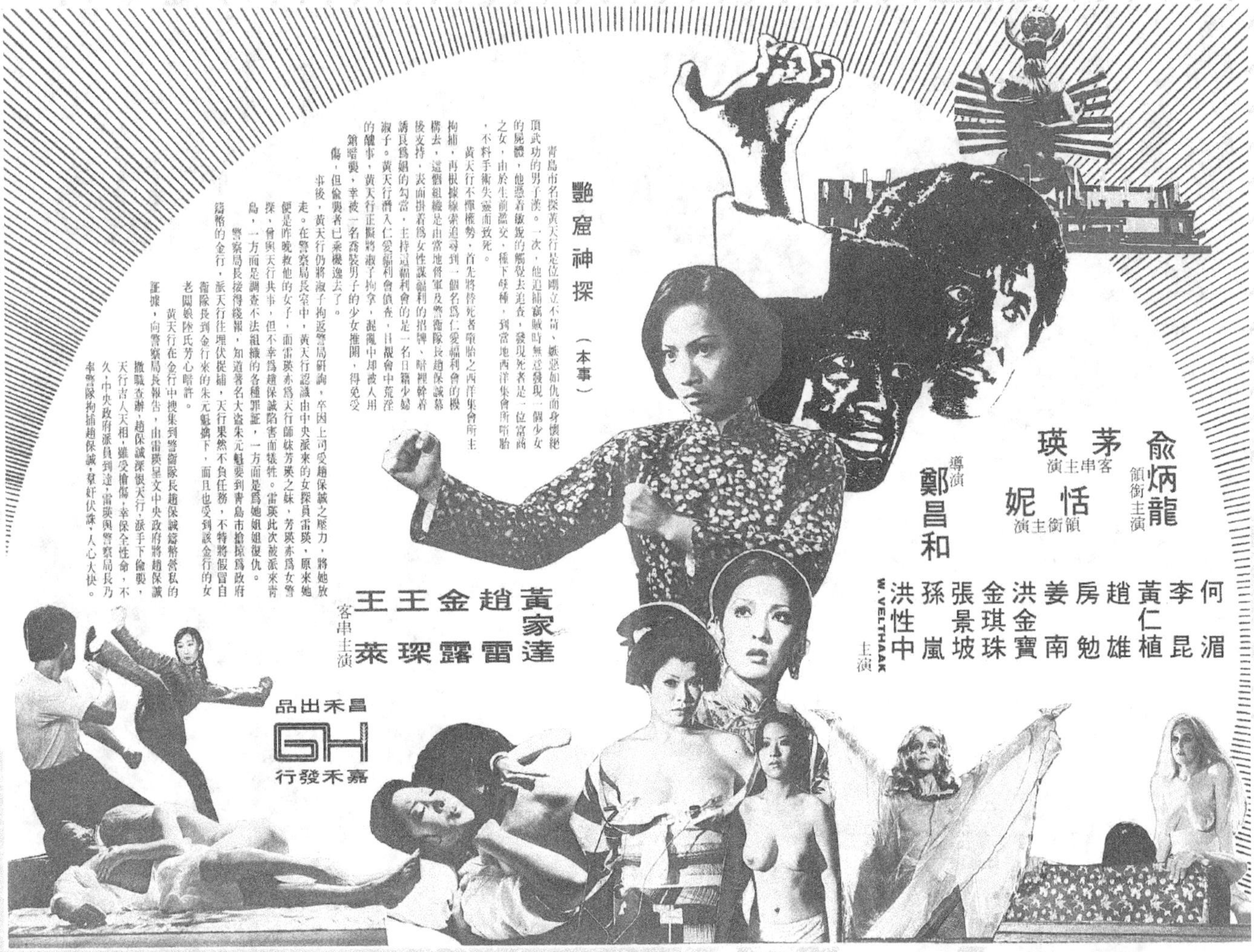

that, and everyone went crazy and were clapping. I was so happy that he invited me to be in his film, and that I could work with such a super star. He said that I only needed to be in one scene, and it would take two days. I said yes. I finished one day and suddenly the director added scenes, it made me film for a whole week.

FD: After you gained popularity in "Enter the Dragon", when did you realise that you became very famous?

AM: Oh never. I never thought about this. I knew that Golden Harvest had to bring up new people like us. I did not know about the US, but I knew about UK. All the big posters. But I never felt I was big and famous. I still had to fully act in my movies.

FD: At the time your movies were constantly being shown at New York's Times Square, did you know about this?

AM: No. I did not know about this.

FD: After "Enter the Dragon" did anyone approach you to film American action movies?

AM: At that time, we were all still new people in the industry. So even if someone were to find us, we wouldn't know. All were managed by the company. The company planned everything.

FD: When was the last time you watched your own movies?

AM: Oh, ha,ha,ha,ha,ha! It has been a few decades; I really didn't watch them. To be honest I knew that I had many fans in America. When I brought my son to Manhattan Park, a stranger asked, "You are Angela Mao?" And I was shocked, I said "Yeah yeah, yeah, yeah, yeah." At the time I knew that oh, I have fans in America too.

FD: It's been about fifty years since your movie career took off, are you surprised that there are still fans that remember you and know who you are?

AM: Yes, it has been fifty years. My son knew a few people from the World Journal (also known as China Daily News) and brought them to the restaurant. They thought I looked familiar and asked him if I was Angela Mao. To be honest we are very humble in America. Even my son's classmates didn't know until my son told them. Their reaction was "No wonder" and they asked me for an interview. I was so surprised that

Starring:
BYONG YU
TIEN NEI

Guest Stars:
ANGELA MAO
CARTER HUANG

Directed By:
CHENG CHANG HO

"THE ASSOCIATION"

Synopsis

Plain-clothe's detective Wang is the best in his trade. And things happen to him fast and thick. One day he stumbles across a young girl's body who apparently has died of abortion. Wang later finds out the abortion is conducted in a foreign club.

Wang arrests the guilty abortionist who leads Wang to a secret organisation called "The Welfare Association". Actually it is an international prostitution racket, forcing innocent young girls into the trade. Wang sneaks into the Association. When he is about to arrest the house madame, a girl in man's disguises saves Wang from certain death.

Wang arrests the madame but has to set her free on orders from above. But Wang is happy to meet his saviour, inspector Lei from headquarters who is here to investigate the secret society, which actually is backed by garrison commander Chao. Lei has an account to settle with Chao too as it is Chao who causes her sister's death.

Wang is successful in trapping the criminal Chu. He has, however, to do his best to ward off the amorous advances from the goldsmith's wife.

But he does learn from her much about the connection between the secret association and Chao. Lei and Wang succeed in getting the commander dismissed. The commander then sends people to kill them. Wang is wounded. With reinforcements, Lei leads the final assault against Chao and his men, she kills Chao, thus avenging her sister's death.

people still know me. Just like now. I really don't know if I should be happy or what. I am thankful and happy that even a few decades later, there are still fans in America and other places in the world that want to know about me, follow me and think of me. So, I am really thankful.

FD: Especially in the UK you have many fans. Out of all your movies which one is your favourite?

AM: My favourite is "Lady Kung Fu", "When Taekwondo Strikes" and "The Fate of Lee Khan"

FD: Now a lot of people want to know where your restaurant is, so they will pay a visit in the hopes of seeing you as they are your fans. Do you ever feel restrained or are you very open to that now?

AM: Oh no, never. I am always open. I was always very plain on my journey. I am very thankful that people still know of me. If you come to eat ay my restaurant, I will thank you. And now my son opened a Cajun Food restaurant that it is also in Bay Side. Just tell my son you want to see me, and I will come.

FD: I have heard about the famous duck you prepare?

AM: I prepare two kinds of ducks every Wednesday for selling them on Friday and the weekends, "Salted Duck" and "Roast Duck". I also sell Soybean Milk on the weekends and the Chef turns up three to four hours before the restaurant open, around 6 am to grind the soy beans to make the milk. We're like the only restaurant in New York that grinds our own soy beans to make the milk instead of using soy milk that's already prepared

FD: Now there are new remastered versions of your movies, did you ever go see them? People say the remastering were beautiful.

AM: For actors like us, we will try our best to perform our characters to the best of our abilities. Sculpt the character in the correct way. I don't dare say I am beautiful. When I was in the movie circle, in opera school, everyone sees me as a boy. Just like Bai Ying. We were basically brothers to everyone.

FD: Did you film "Hapkido" and "Lady Whirlwind" at the same time or "Hapkido" and then "Lady Whirlwind"?

AM: It was "Lady Whirlwind" first. It was with "When Taekwondo Strikes". I entered Golden Harvest in 1970 so in 1971 I filmed both movies in South Korea. Some scenes were also filmed back in Hong Kong.

FD: "Lady Whirlwind" was shown two and a half months after the "Fist of Fury" (or "Chinese Connection"), but when you filmed this movie Bruce Lee was not famous yet. Is this correct?

AM: It is hard to say but at the time Bruce Lee was already famous in Hollywood. But he was new in Golden Harvest. He went to Thailand to film the "Big Boss". "Lady Whirlwind" was then stored and then shown to the public after the "Big Boss" and "Fist of Fury".

FD: But these movies were all made at the same time?

AM: Yes, they were made at about the same time. In fact, I rode the wave of Bruce Lee at the time.

FD: Some say the "Lady Whirlwind" had a touch of Italian taste to it (Spaghetti Western). It is different to the movies before, containing themes like revenge and having lots of outdoor scenes. Every scene was long and there wasn't much dialogue, especially your character.

AM: Yes, my character was like a Chinese police officer. For example, there was drug dealing. In "Lady Whirlwind" I pretended to be a male character. I still remember that vividly.

FD: Your hair was very short.

AM: Yes, yes, my hair was cut into an Audrey Hepburn style of hair.

FD: In many scenes you appear suddenly, like a ghost. In the movie you were seeking revenge for your sister. Your character was actively seeking revenge for your sister who was killed by Ling Shi-Hua played by Cheng Yi, so as the older sister you had to seek revenge.

AM: That was not "Lady Whirlwind", was it?

導演 鄭昌和　主演 韓英傑　何湄　洪金寶　石允天　李中　王萊　司馬華龍　魯俊　夏雨　張佩山　方野　趙雄 ·主演·

BROKE

嘉禾貢獻
最佳影片
鄒文懷 監製
茅瑛 領銜主演
梁小龍 陳惠敏 領銜主演
特別介紹白眉派高手
郭振猷 關山 特別客串

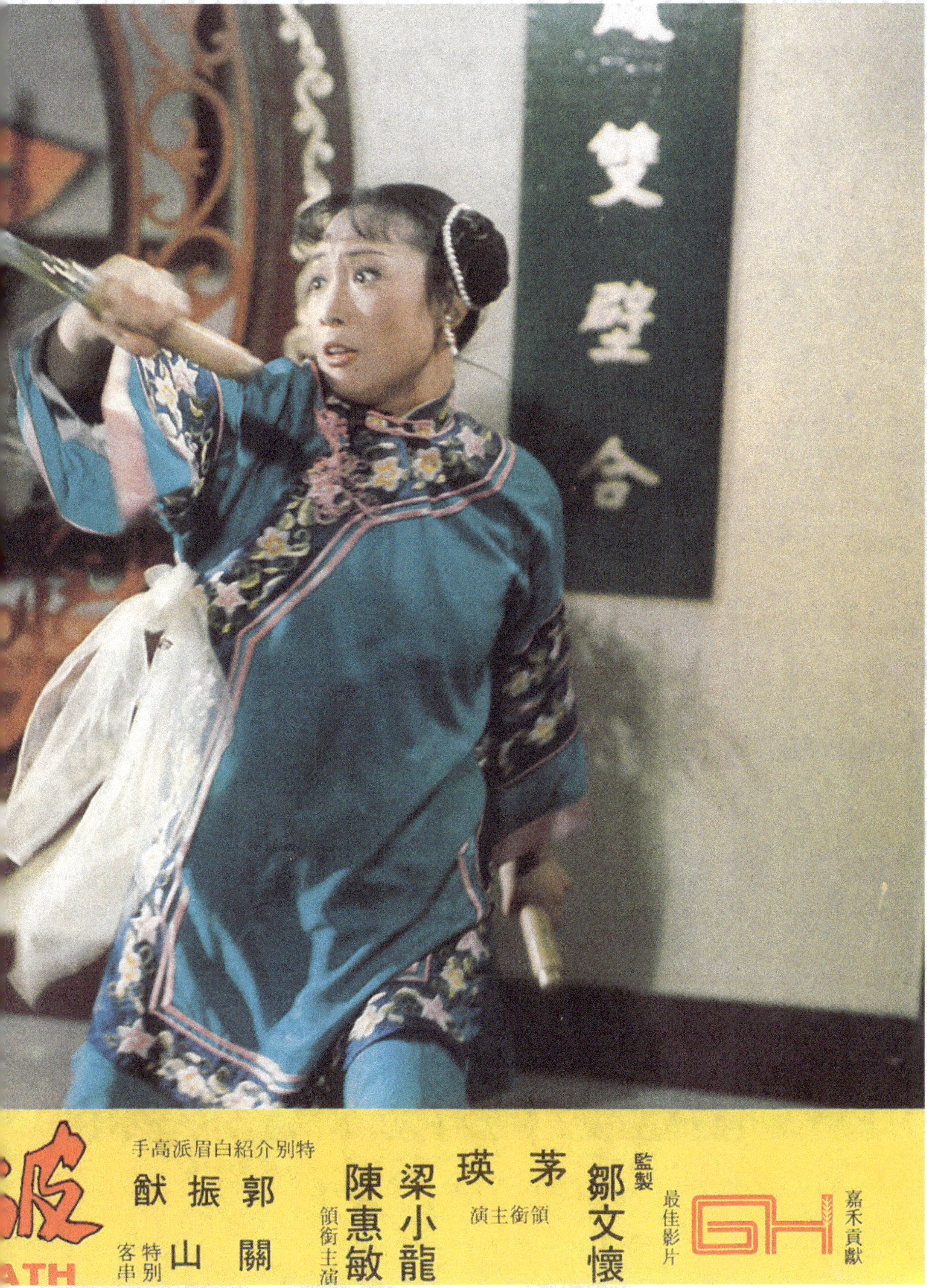

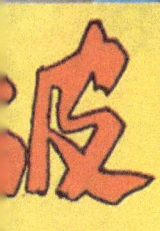

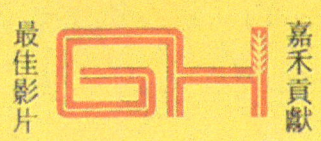

FD: Yes, it is "Lady Whirlwind"!

AM: Oh, oh, oh, yes, maybe the translation is different.

FD: The movie had many other names like "Deep Thrust" so maybe that confused you?

AM: That is probably the reason. Yes, yes, yes.

FD: Your character was seeking revenge for the sister. Did director Huang Feng talk to you about this character?

AM: It was not just director Huang Feng. Every director must talk to their actors and other members of staff. The director gathered all of them to talk about the details of each character. It doesn't just include the background. It includes things like lighting when certain things happen at where. This was all prep work. The tradition must be done and was passed on from prior movies.

FD: Did director Huang Feng talk to you about the style of the movie being similar to western (cowboy) films and how he wanted to present it?

AM: Of course. At the time when I was filming "Lady Whirlwind" and "When Taekwondo Strikes" I was still new in Golden Harvest and the movie circle. I entered in 1970 with "The Angry River" and at the time it was 1971, I was still new. This meant that he had to talk to me and everyone about the special characters and special moves. So, we had to practice. For example, I remember that in one scene I was in a submarine, and I had to swim, going down and wearing a diving suit. I did not know how to swim! It was not like I did not know how to swim per-se. I could swim for a few steps only. And I had to carry the oxygen tank in the movie. That was so tough. It was filmed in the winter. It was really tough.

FD: I remember seeing the movie and knowing it was filmed in the winter as I could see the breath when the characters were having a conversation.

AM: Yes, yes.

FD: Why did so many of these Kung Fu movies shot in South Korea?

AM: I honestly don't know. Maybe it was cheaper to film there. Thinking about it now, South Korea had lots of buildings with architecture similar to mainland China. So maybe it was filmed there for this reason.

FD: Were there any issues in terms of communication with the South Korean staff?

AM: We used sign language and body language. Sometimes we used English and other ways to communicate. When it came to lines, we said our lines, and they said their lines. As actors we had to not just remember our own lines but also memorize the lines of the other characters. You needed to remember their specific lines, which were your signal to start speaking. This will cause the movie and scene to evoke emotion and seem lively.

FD: At the time they spoke Korean and you spoke Mandarin?

AM: Yes, yes, yes.

FD: Do you still remember where majority of "Lady Whirlwind" was filmed in South Korea?

AM: "Lady Whirlwind" had a lot of outdoor scenes, but I can't really remember them. Lots of scenes were filmed in Hong Kong, including the submarine scene

(Angela may have confused "Lady Whirlwind" with "When Taekwondo Strikes").

FD: Were the fight scenes with Chang Yi filmed in Hong Kong?

AM: Yes.

FD: Does that mean that some of the actors did not go to South Korea?

AM: Yes, not all the actors went to South Korea. As a director you had to know which scenes were going to be filmed in a foreign place, which actors to bring and what machinery is needed. When they come back, everyone is back together.

FD: In total how much time was spent in South Korea for filming?

AM: At that time many scenes were filmed in South Korea. The time spent there was just enough to film "Lady Whirlwind" and "When Taekwondo Strikes". "When Taekwondo Strikes" was filmed first, and "Lady Whirlwind" was filmed after.

FD: You don't remember how much time you spent in South Korea?

AM: Oh, I stayed there for a year and a half. I learned Hapkido there. We filmed in morning and had nothing to eat. So, I became the chef in the hotel. They bought the ingredients. Sammo Hung and I had an electric cooker, and we cooked the food and we ate at night. At the time Chang Yi, Sammo and I went to learn Hapkido. In one year and a half, we got 3rd degree black belt. It was around 1971 to 1972.

FD: How is Chang Yi as an actor? In this movie he did not play an antagonist, but more of a good person.

AM: Oh, Chang Yi is too familiar to me. We grew up together in the Opera School. He is a great actor we both tried very hard. We are too close to him.

FD: Are you still in contact with him?

AM: Yes, he is in Vancouver right now, we still talk through WeChat. We all have contacts with our opera classmates, even the ones who are still in Taiwan. We have known each other for 63 years now.

FD: Other than Chang Yi, we also want to know your opinion of Carter Wong (Huang Jia Da).

AM: He was a great actor; I was the one to bring him into Golden Harvest.

FD: We will talk about him later. So, Sammo Hung was the antagonist in the movie, and you had many fight scenes with him. Were the fight scenes choreographed on the day or was it planned ahead?

AM: For every movie it had to be planned and everyone had to know that beforehand. Since I had the background and knowledge on this, I did not need it as much. But for many actors who didn't have this background, the fight choreographers would have to give them lessons and teach them what to do. Since we were so familiar as we all came from Beijing Opera, they gave me the requirements on the day. If they were the not the same, we would be familiar anyway. They told me what to do on the day and I would just know how to do it. This also included Hapkido foot work and kicks.

FD: Did you then give suggestions to add things or change things so the fight scene would be better?

AM: Of course, I gave suggestions because everyone's move, front side and back side would be different. We talked about it and discussed to create the best possible scenes, so everyone is comfortable with what they are doing. It depends on the director and of course the camera. If it looked good on camera it was ok. This is how we unite during and after one movie.

FD: In this movie you had lots of action scenes; do you have a favourite out of all?

AM: Which one are you talking about?

FD: "Lady Whirlwind".

AM: Oh, that I don't remember, I only remember "Lady Kung Fu" ("Hapkido").

FD: At the end of "Lady Whirlwind", your character let the character of Chang Yi free. It seemed that you were touched by his righteousness and justice, so you let him and his fiancée leave. Was this planned since the start of the movie or was it a last-minute decision by the director?

AM: To be honest, I don't really remember "Lady Whirlwind", I only remember the submarine scene. I still have the tape at home and can rewatch the tape. I don't really remember. "Lady Kung Fu" is the one I remember the best.

FD: Anything you want to add from the questions we talked about before?

AM: Just ask me questions and I will answer as I remember as it had been a few decades.

FD: When "Lady Kung Fu" (Hapkido) was shown, it had already been half a year after "The Fist of Fury. Lady Kung Fu had many similar scenes and fight choreography to Fist of Fury. Was this due to the success of Fist of Fury?

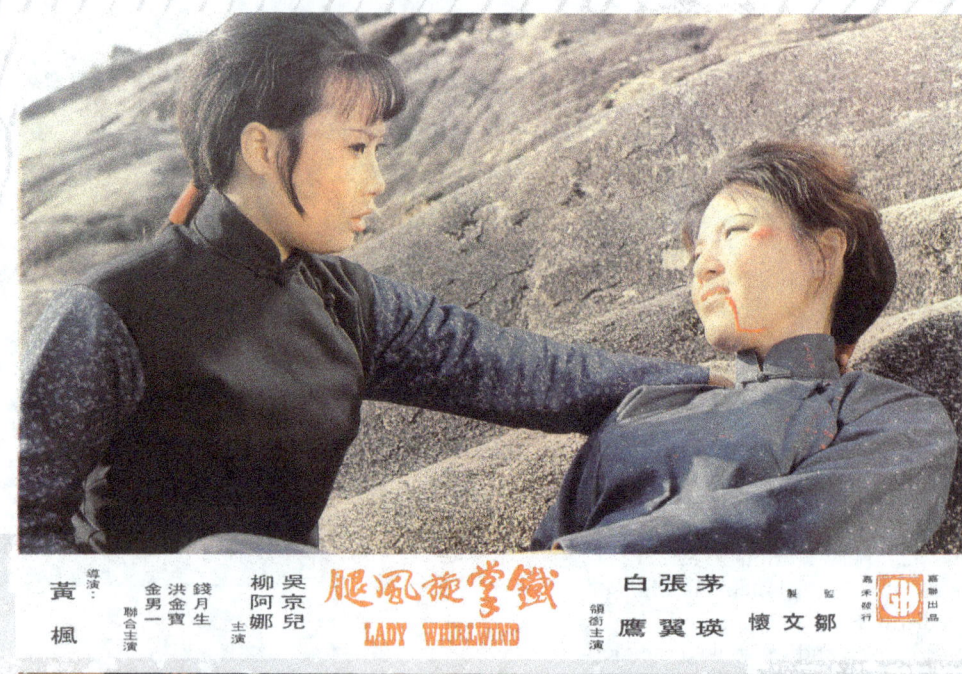

AM: This I don't know. I only knew about the story when I received the script. When it comes to scenes, well yes, because both films looked at problems between China and Japan, both had settings in dojos, both had the theme of revenge. We were Chinese; the Japanese did bad things to us and now we had to do something back. Whether male or female, there were fights in the dojo. I remember about one shot that I filmed in the dojo. That shot was taken 52 times. It was a spinning kick. It was really hard. I kept doing the spinning kick, spinning, and kicking, spinning, and kicking, I did it fifty-two times and I ended up being so tired that I just sat there right after the shot. I remember this shot best.

FD: When "Lady Kung Fu" was being produced, the "Fist of Fury" was already shown to the public.

AM: Well, both were produced at around the same time. It was after Bruce Lee filmed "The Big Boss", he wanted to make "The Fist of Fury". After "The Fist of Fury" was shown, "Lady Kung Fu" had already been finished. When Bruce Lee came to invite me to play a role in his movie ("Enter the Dragon"), I was at the production studio filming "Lady Kung Fu". He asked me personally to play his sister.

FD: At that time did you have your black belt?

AM: Yes, I had my black belt at the time.

FD: Except "Hapkido", did you have to practice anything else to film the movie?

鐵掌旋風腿 LADY WHIRLWIND

鐵掌旋風腿 LADY WHIRLWIND

導演: 黃楓　聯合主演 錢月生 洪金寶 金男一　主演 柳阿娜 吳京兒　腿風旋掌鐵 LADY WHIRLWIND　領銜主演 白鷹 張翼 茅瑛　監製 鄒文懷　嘉禾發行 嘉聯出品

導演: 黃楓　聯合主演 錢月生 洪金寶 金男一　主演 柳阿娜 吳京兒　腿風旋掌鐵 LADY WHIRLWIND　領銜主演 白鷹 張翼 茅瑛　監製 鄒文懷　嘉禾發行 嘉聯出品

Page 32　Eastern Heroes Angela Mao Special

AM: Not specially. I trained daily on Chinese Opera moves. When I woke up and opened my eyes, I stretch, I kick, I do everything I can do. Even now I still do these things. When I wash dishes, I stretch at the same time. This is because no matter how old you are, your flexibility and tendons are the most important. If your tendons hurt, you can no longer walk. Learning these moves is not to be used in fights, it is to create a healthy body and have a longer life. If you train properly, your tendons and muscles will be healthy as ever and no matter how old you are you will not look old.

FD: Many of your movies were filmed with Li You Tang.

AM: Yes, he was a cinematographer.

FD: How familiar is he to you, and how much do you remember about him?

AM: He was a great cinematographer. He was a guru. I think he was brought (by the founders) to Golden Harvest from Shaw Brothers alongside director Huang Feng. Cinematography is not my area of specialty and not my profession, but the cinematographer, director, and fight choreographer will decide where to place the camera and at what angles. He was great. He would always say in Cantonese, "Ms. Mao, your foot cannot be seen here, it has to tilt or curve towards this side." In that way the kick will look even better so if you want a good scene. No matter how good your move was, if the camera doesn't catch it well, it will be different and not as good. This is one of the tips and tricks in making a good movie.

FD: What do you think was the biggest change in style in this movie compared to the other ones done by Director Huang Feng?

AM: What do you mean here?

FD: It feels like the style changed in "Lady Kung Fu".

ALTERNATIVE COVER IMAGE

AM: Do you mean in the later stages?

FD: Yes.

AM: No, the fact is that every director cannot have only one fixed style. Once in a while, because of business, they have to follow what the community and society wants. Just like us actors, we can't keep doing the same thing. We can't keep staying in these Kung Fu movies. However, I wasn't there too long. After 10 years I was married and I quitted as an actor.

FD: When you trained Hapkido, you practiced with the founder Ji Han Jae. Did you have any difficulties?

AM: Well, he was my master (my Sifu), my master in Hapkido.

FD: At the time did director Huang Feng say that he (Ji Han Jae) could play a minor role in the movie? As he was not an actor after all.

AM: He was not an actor. He had a dojo in South Korea and the three of us went to practice Hapkido there.

FD: And there was Hwang In-Shik?

AM: Yes, Hwang In-Shik was our senior. He was impressive, he was 7th degree in Hapkido. 7th degree black belt. He could fly over ten people and then land one side kick; this was all real.

FD: And when they filmed this movie, they spoke Korean?

AM: Yes, yes, yes.

FD: You filmed many movies with Bai Ying, including "Lady Kung Fu". How is he as a friend and as an actor?

AM: As an actor he was dedicated, and he was a good friend. He was a big brother to me. He is in Hong Kong now and we still speak with each other.

FD: Oh, he is still in Hong Kong; he must be 80 now right?

AM: Uh, I don't think so. I think he is just shy of 80. His movies were all first class. When we were filming "The Fate of Lee Khan", we had to film a scene on a white top mountain and we had to take a boat to cross the river. He held onto me the whole time. He called me "brother", at the time I was twenty and still a bit chubby, and my personality was like a boy.

FD: That was the first movie of Carter Wong. Did you think he was nervous, or did he already show signs of being a great commander-like character?

AM: He came from a background of karate. He had scars all over his hands. Doing karate made his body was stiffer, but apart from that karate is practically the same with other martial arts. Carter was decent. People did things differently, but he acted decently. As an actor he did not have much emotion. Usually, as an actor you have to be lively with your emotions. You had to have a lot of movement on your face and not be very stiff. If you were stiff in front of the camera it was not very convincing. It just took time, just like when I started in the movie industry. It took some time to slowly change those habits that I picked up from Chinese opera. It took practice and honing. Every actor is honed through time.

FD: At the start of the movie, it felt like you were holding back. In the first hour, there were many scenes that you seemed to control and contain yourself from fights, and only started fighting in the last 30 minutes. The last thirty minutes was just straight fighting. Was this planned at all from the start?

AM: It depends on personality of the character. Every character has their own way of doing things. In "Hapkido" Carter was playing my senior. His character was more of a hothead, and my character tended to talk more. When I really couldn't hold myself back, I would go all out and fight. For his character that just took one dispute.

FD: So, he was the hothead and you were the calm one.
AM: Wait. Did he play my senior? I really can't remember as these people were in basically all of my movies and playing different characters. It has been a few decades and I really can't remember who is who.

FD: Sammo Hung was also the fight chorographer of "Lady Kung Fu", was there any reason why?

AM: Well, Sammo Hung, Chang Yi and I all came from the Chinese Opera background. But since we were doing a film based in the early days of the Chinese Republic, our fight scenes needed to be grand. What we knew was not the prettiest, so we had to go learn Hapkido to present the prettiest and grandest moves in the film. This could not have been achieved in another way like changing camera angles. All of our kicks and punches all looked fabulous.

FD: You had a fight scene using an umbrella, right?

AM: Yes, an umbrella and a pigtail.

FD: Did you learn to use these two techniques before, or did you learn them for this movie?

AM: To be honest, I never learned how to use the pigtail. It was very last minute and used for effects. But the umbrella was always used in Opera School. It was like: oh, your pigtails could be used, and then some ball-shaped things were added to them so they could be used as a weapon and effect. It was all last minute.

FD: Was using an umbrella Sammo Hung's idea?

AM: Yes

FD: And it was done on the spot?

AM: Yes, in many situations he made decisions on the fly. "Oh, that can be used, this can be used." Then those props would be used on the set.

FD: A lot of Sammo Hung's fellows have been stuntmen or participated in your movies, did you communicate with those people, and do you remember your interactions?

AM: Since we all came from Chinese Opera, we understood what each other was saying. We are like a family, like brothers and sisters. We could always have lunch together, have a coffee have a drink, even though I didn't drink alcohol. I would just have a coffee with them. It was just like

Bruce Lee. He treated all of us under him very well, to be honest with you. We were very united.

FD: Most of the scenes were filmed in South Korea, and one of the actors was Goro Kumon. He was Japanese. Do you know if he was in any other movies or did, he stop after just one? How was your interaction and collaboration with him?

AM: It wasn't too bad, wasn't too bad.

FD: But he only spoke English and not Chinese?

AM: He spoke both Japanese and English, but our English was not very good at the time. We had to take it slowly. However, everyone was having fun in the production studio. People were learning English, Cantonese, Chinese. Everyone got along. There were conversations between actors and backstage staff like the audio staff, the costume staff, and other members. Everyone got along well.

FD: "Lady Kung Fu" had many fight scenes, which was your favourite?

AM: It would be the last scene. In the last scene I jumped onto a trampoline and side kicked Bai Ying's character to death. Then I strangled another one to death with my pigtail. That shot was done like thirty or forty times. I learned how to use a trampoline just for this movie. I had to because the camera was high up. It had to see your face and the kick close up.

FD: Last question, since this year is the 50th anniversary for these films, and "The Fist of Fury".

AM: Wow, it has already been fifty years! I never thought about that. Right now, I am old, and time just passes by.

FD: For these movies people call you "The Queen of Martial Art", "The First Queen of Action Films".

AM: Thank you, thank you.

FD: Many people think even fifty years later these are really good action films, any final thoughts?

AM: To be honest I did not think it has been fifty years. I am just grateful. I just want to say on behalf of myself and Bruce Lee, thank you too all the movie fans. Even fifty years later you can still remember us. Thank you thank you. At last, I would wish everyone good health and take care!
After speaking with Angela, Frank had a chance to catch up with Thomas, Angela's eldest son. Over to Frank and Thomas.

 嘉禾貢獻 最佳影片 編導 黃楓 雷偉民 韓英傑 姜南 馮毅 張亦飛 李家鼎 聯合主演 **鬼怒川 THE ANGRY RIVER** 茅瑛 高遠 白鷹 領銜主演 監製 鄒文懷  嘉禾貢獻 最佳影片

 嘉禾貢獻 最佳影片 編導 黃楓 雷偉民 韓英傑 姜南 馮毅 張亦飛 李家鼎 聯合主演 **鬼怒川 THE ANGRY RIVER** 茅瑛 高遠 白鷹 領銜主演 監製 鄒文懷  嘉禾貢獻 最佳影片

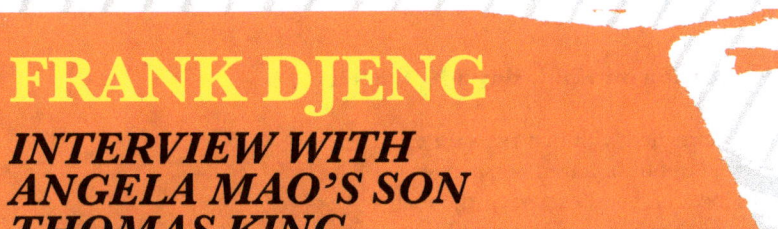

FRANK DJENG
INTERVIEW WITH ANGELA MAO'S SON THOMAS KING

FD: I am here with Thomas King, one of Angela Mao's sons, and we're going to talk about what happened to the Queen of Martial Arts? Well, she ended up in Queens, New York. Can you tell me how it all started, how your family ended up here, and how it leads to the restaurant?

TK: We emigrated from Taiwan (1983). When I was seven, my younger brother, George, was still in womb, and we emigrated from Taipei, Taiwan over to New York City. Honestly at seven years old I didn't know why we came. Initially it was a bit of a struggle. I remember going from a house basically to then living in a small room for four in Chinatown right on Mott Street. It was a big change but, at the same time now looking back, I understood why. Better opportunities for us the younger generations. That's my guess at that's why they did it.

I didn't fully understand the magnitude of my mom's fame. Again, when you're young, you don't really think about those things. She was always just "Mom" so that's why the sacrifice means more now.

FD: So you guys came here into New York whilst staying in Mott Street in Chinatown, is that where the first restaurant started?

TK: No, that's not. So we were in Mott Street Chinatown and the 1980's as you may or may not know, was not a good time for Chinatown. It was not a place where you would want to raise a young person, young man, especially at seven years old. The criminal element was a little too rough. So, we moved out, we went out to Elmhurst, jumped around Elmhurst, Jackson Heights, Corona and…restaurants started when I turned about 14 years old.

The very first restaurant was on Roosevelt Avenue between Prince and College Point and it was called "Mama King" named after my Grandmother.

FD: Was that in Flushing?

TK: Yes, it was in Flushing. It was in downtown Flushing and from there on it just kind of evolved and moved and now we have the Chinese restaurant in this name, in Chinese Nan Bei Ho which means "Harmony between North and South". We have had this restaurant since I was 17 years old. I am 46 now, so almost 30 years.

FD: But the original location was in Flushing?

TK: The original location was in Flushing, the first Nan Bei Ho was, well it wasn't called "Nan Bei Ho" yet but it was over where the Library is now. I forget what that road is, but it's on Main Street and right by the Library. It used to be called "☐☐☐" which literally means "The One and Only Place". So from there, we moved over to 40th Row and that's when the name "Nan Bei Ho" got suggested.

FD: Who came up with the name "Nan Bei Ho"?

TK: My eldest Uncle. The patriarch of the family since my grandfather passed. He came up with the name and then from then on, and he's been the staple in Flushing as a restaurateur. So when he said "Hey, I want this restaurant this name", it kind of stuck. And we were there for, I'd say, 15 / 17 years. Quite a long time.

FD: What was the decision behind doing Taiwanese cooking? Has it always been the idea? To get to like, when we do the restaurant we're going to do full Taiwanese cooking?

TK: One of the main reasons is that when we first moved here to Queens, there were literally one or two restaurants that we would go and eat. My mom would say "I don't wanna cook for anyone, let's go out". We only had two choices, and they were both in Flushing. One was more of a breakfast place and the other. So my father always had that idea like "we wanna do something", "we wanna have some place we can go". My Uncle, my oldest Uncle being a restaurateur, came up with the ideas and my other Uncles came there and said "Yeah, let's do it, let's make something".

We were all born in Taiwan so that was the cuisine we grew up with, but we also have roots back in China, Northern China, so you know, North / South, that's how that came about.

FD: When did the restaurant move to the current location on 42nd, Bayside, Queens?

TK: About fifteen years ago. That's when we moved and it coincided with that real estate boom in 2006 or 2007 or so. Long story short; we were priced out from a rent perspective. We thought we couldn't really survive there. We found this location and because of the real estate boom a lot of Asians, Chinese, Taiwanese moved out to this area, we thought "Let's follow them, let's go with this flow".

We came here fifteen years ago and the first few years were kind of tough. We weren't quite sure where we moved to, I don't know them, this is a new place, and there was some confusion. But then they saw my Mom and they saw my Dad and said "Oh you're the same place!" So they were like "You're the same people from Mama King, The One and Only Place and Nan Bei Ho in Flushing"; then everybody started coming here. We were very lucky from that perspective.

FD: The food over there was great, I've been there several times and I always enjoyed it and it was always fun about how your Mom would talk about the specialties, bean curd and the soy milk, could you talk a bit about the dedication, the time is spent, the care and the quality?

TK: It stems from our love of food and the way Mom and my Dad were taught and would think about the food. Where my Grandmother, God rest her soul, when she was alive, the care she took and that's the way my Father remembers and that is the way my Mother was taught. So when we, I say "we" loosely because I don't do that, when we started the restaurant, we needed individuals who are as dedicated as we are, who are as strict with the flavours, the methods, and the steps as we are. That was where this came from. A lot of the folks that have been with us for twenty / thirty years, the chefs; we have also have waitresses that started when they were nineteen and have been here twenty plus years. It's a family but everyone is dedicated to their craft.

FD: Like your Mom talks about the bean curd, the soy milk, you only make three or four barrels as it takes hours.

ALTERNATIVE COVER IMAGE

TK: Yeah, so I don't want to criticise other places, but they don't use fresh soy beans, we actually grind them so we can cook them downstairs. Not just the soy bean milk, the soft soy bean soup, the sweet soup, we make our own dumplings, soup dumplings; That dedication is hard to find but it is also kind of hard to replace. God forbid something happens, yes but it would be very hard to replace as when we look to the future we want to persevere.

FD: Like today, when we were interviewing your Mom, she's here today to make that duck! She comes in once a week to make this duck that takes like hours of preparation?

TK: Yeah the braised duck that she makes. I don't eat the duck cos for me, it's work! Cos it's off the bone. You have to eat it with the bone. The sauce she makes it in, I mean, I could eat three or four for bowls of rice with that, easy. I don't need anything else but that.

FD: And that place has consistently done well, right?

TK: Consistently, 'knock on wood' right, one of the big things is we had people my age who were brought to the Flushing restaurant, at my age, when I was young like thirteen, fourteen, fifteen, now are my age and they are bringing their kids, so it's kind of life multi-generational and they keep coming back. One of the main reasons for that is consistency. The flavour is consistent, you know when you go there and order a three-cooked chicken, or even General Tso's chicken, or you order something more specialty like □□(Numbing spicy) sticky tofu, it's that flavour. It's that flavour you remember from thirty years ago, it's that flavour you remember from twenty years ago, so that's one of the things.

FD: One of our cameramen had General Tso's chicken, he said it's the best chicken he's ever had.

TK: Thank you.

FD: Now obviously for the last two years Covid has wreaked havoc on a lot of things. Has Covid had an effect on your business? Was the restaurant closed during Covid? And you had to resort to just take-out?

TK: Yeah, so basically what happened when, well it affected a lot of people right, everyone was affected, so we closed for about two and half to three weeks. Simply because it was at the height, a lot safety measures weren't really in place and no mask mandates, and no vaccine, so a lot that hindered the business. For a restaurant you obviously have to have people, you have to have people in chairs ordering your food, or waitresses that depend on tips and obviously wages for our chefs as well. We decided to shut down for two to three weeks and we reopen with new plastic protection, alcohol cleaners, hand sanitisers, and to your point, we restricted it to take-out only.

We actually got so much support from our customers because we still made all those things they became dependent on weekends and we still had those things available so they really reached out and said "We need you to stay around" and "We'll support you".

FD: Were there long lines for it?

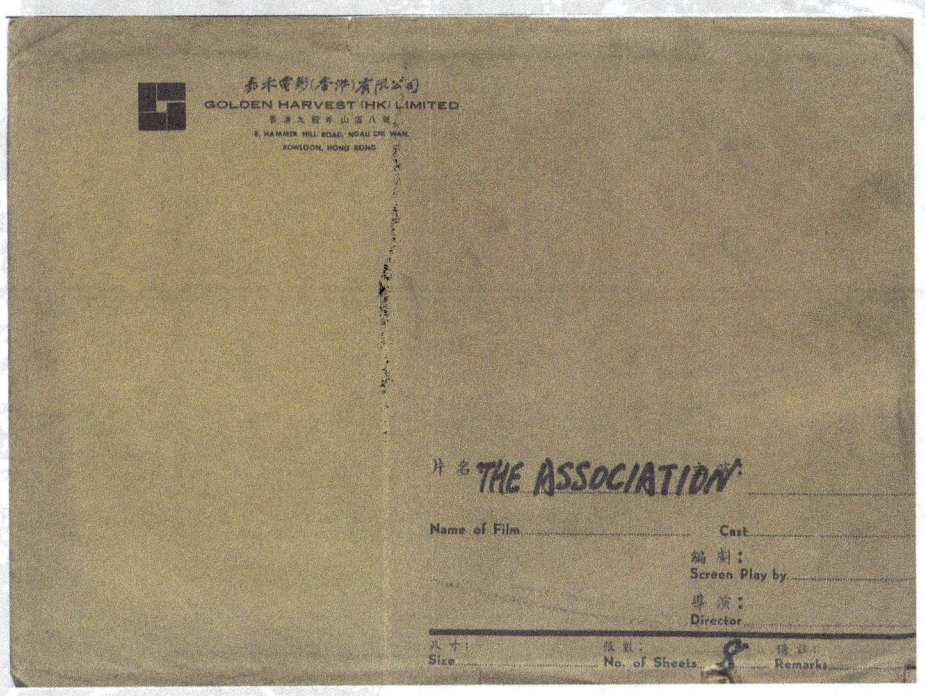

TK: Ha, so yeah actually we had very long lines on weekends and people were taking out. They even ordered extra as a show of support and to say "we love your food" and "we need you to stick around". We feel really loved and supported.

FD: That's pretty amazing, but even more amazing was this place that we're here, "The Shack", you guys basically opened this restaurant during the pandemic. How did this place come up? The last time I was here interviewing your mum for a documentary I was working on, still working on actually, it was a hotpot place! How did a hotpot place turn into "The Shack"?

TK: So the hotpot place was something that my brother had an idea about bringing Taiwanese stone hotpot to Queens. Unfortunately he was probably two years ahead of time. We were two years ahead of the curve and in the restaurant world that's like light years as you don't have the customer base, the demographics really don't

 **"THE ASSOCIATION"** COLOUR SCOPE

 **"THE ASSOCIATION"** COLOUR SCOPE

"THE ASSOCIATION" COLOUR SCOPE
GH Golden Harvest Presents

reflect that here. It was a really good idea but we still get some traction and, not to belittle the point, but our personal health issues and family statuses, really didn't help us in the terms we reacted to work. We had to unfortunately shut the place down.

So fast forward a couple years what we then did was, "We want to do something more" we still want to be the local neighbourhood spot that everybody goes to, everybody is aware of. At the same time, we felt like we had more to give. We want to bring other cuisine to this place and this area. One of the things, we very fortuitously met a couple of chefs. One had trained down South for ten or eleven years, so he knows that southern Cajun grill style cooking and another friend of ours he had trained at a culinary school, so put that together with us coming from a cooking background, family, a restaurant family. We thought "let's do something", "Let's pull something together". Have some kind of flavour that no one has done up here is really doing. That's how "The Shack" came about.

FD: No one does this over on our side; I'm from the Bay area, the West coast. We don't have anything like this as it seems it is a homey community, a family place where you come, relax, eat your food and chat with the 'crew', basically the staff here, and have a good time. Was that the idea all along?

TK: Yeah, so that's like the idea. It's really like, we call it "Southern Inspired" So in reality what we we're really looking for is comfort food. Some place you can bring your family and just hang out, maybe the Mom and Dad have a few drinks, the kids can have an ice cream at the end. Just have some good food, some comfort food.

We also want to be the place you can bring a date and you don't feel pretentious or you don't feel overwhelmed or like you have to order 'this' and have to do 'that', but somewhere really comfortable. Somewhere you can sit for hours and again converse and catch up with your friends and just socialise.

FD: The quality is great and the steak is fantastic, all the different combos, the boiled seafood combo, they're great, the appetizers are fantastic, I wish we had somewhere like here on the West Coast.

Going back to Nan Bei Ho for a second, you have mentioned how the place has now been around for close to thirty years. What are some of the issues continuing the longevity of the place? You talk about the chefs, I am sure the chefs are getting up there in age, so…

TK: The biggest thing is consistency. Making sure the flavour profile is consistent. That's more from an internal side. I think from a food

"THE ASSOCIATION" COLOUR SCOPE

perspective it is the consistency of the food, the quality of the food, where we get our produce from, our meats etc., so that is something that we need to control.

To your point, our chefs are getting up there in age; they have been there a long time. It is passing that down to the next generation. The willingness to teach the next generation and the willingness of the next generation to learn and to follows those steps and be what we need them to be. That is a challenge. It is a challenge we can overcome, you just find the right individuals with the right talent, and you're good.

The external ones are a little more difficult to control. Demographics of the area, additionally I think food costs, rising inflation unfortunately something we cannot really control. We kind of have to roll with that, if you will.

I would say those are the two biggest things that we need to be cognitive of and really understand how we move forward in that space.

FD: There are similar sort of issues at play in, say, Canada too. All the Hong Kong immigrants that went there in 1980's, Vancouver, Toronto they went to open restaurants, started cooking, food with good quality ingredients but now, it's like they're in the 70's...

TK: Yes, and they're retiring and you're losing that entire generation's flavour. That's the tough thing. It's like how do we continue that for the next generation? In teaching them, it is also a two-way street. They have to be willing to learn it and vice versa; we have to be willing to teach them and be patient in that.

It's a tough proposition but at the same time, I think you can still find a middle ground and continue it forward.

FD: Let's talk about your Mom for a little bit. When did you and your brother become aware she had this previous career?
TK: So I've always known my Mom was an actress and I've always know she's a martial artist because she used to try and teach us when we were young; the horse stance, all these different moves. I'm sorry to say we were not as blessed as she was in terms of physical ability so we gave up on that and she focused on schooling and other trades. I realised my Mom was famous when, I don't know if you know but, New York had some Saturday afternoon or Sunday afternoon matinee TV.

FD: "Black Belt Theatre"?

TK: Something like that, it was similar to that; but it was "Saturday Afternoon Kung Fu Matinees" or something; "The Five Deadly Venoms",

 **"THE ASSOCIATION"**
COLOUR SCOPE

 **"THE ASSOCIATION"**
COLOUR SCOPE

 "THE ASSOCIATION" COLOUR SCOPE
GOLDEN HARVEST PRESENTS

"36 Chambers of Shaolin" and things like that. One day I was at home with my friends and "Enter The Dragon" comes on. All my friends are watching the TV and they were like watching the TV and then they looked at me… and they looked at me again. "Wait a minute! That's your Mom! What's she doing on TV with Bruce Lee? How come you guys don't tell us. You haven't even told me?" I'm like "That's just Mom!" Right? Not to be sensational but she disciplines me, she yells at me, to me, that's just Mom. It doesn't matter whether she is in a movie with Bruce Lee. It's Mom.

From then on I kind of realised that she is famous but again, I'm not the one who's famous it's her.

That was the first instance; the second instance was one of the restaurants we had over by the library, a movie buff came in with all these billboards and posters, the laser discs. He came in like "Where's Angela Mao?" I said "Who are you?" I didn't want to say anything at the time as she was in the back. He then said "I am so-and-so, I collect these things, I do not sell them, and can I do this?

That's when I realised "Wow! She is that famous!"

FD: Were you aware that, like, her movies are shown in Times Square and 42nd Street year after year, we asked her just now and she said she didn't know.

TK: Yes, none of us knew. We were invited a few years back a screening of "Enter the Dragon", "Hapkido", or something in downtown Chinatown movie theatre and this was the third time I realise and finally realise the whole magnitude of her fame. I went to the theatre and there were about four hundred people there. The line we had for her signature, I just looked and I was dumb founded. "What is going on!?" What really struck me, people we like "Let me get a picture of you too!" and I was like "But I'm not famous!" "No, but your Mom is famous!... And I can now say I know her son!" So I'm like "Wow" It's the precedence of property, well ok, she's the one famous, I am not famous so. So that's where we are in terms of her fame. Now I fully understand where her fame is.

FD: Has her own perception of her legacy changed over the years? The general consensus or perception was that she would shy away for a long time. It seems over the recent years she has become more acceptable. Why do you think that's the case?

TK: I think one of the big things is Hector Martinez is one of the reasons she has become more open and accepting of some of this attention if you will. Hector came from a very respectful angle. "I'm not here to hound you for an autograph, I'm here because you are one of my heroes" He then brought other individuals that had that same mindset.

Even though they know she's here, they are not here every day. They respect her space and her life. She has seen more people like that, yourself included, and has seen a lot more people like that, she is more open to it. There are individuals also in that circle that have reached out and asked if she can be a cameo in a film or a short film and she's more open to it now. "As long as you're doing a good story, I'll think about it". So she's a lot more open to it and I think it has to do with fans nowadays, especially the older generation, like us, coming to her from a very respectful angle.

Not like some of these fans that have almost like a stalker-ish kind of feel. They're more like "I know where she is, she's a friend of mine, you wanna see her? I'm gonna have to check first, we'll meet in public" and not just like "I'll just take you" but "Let me check with her, let me make sure she's ok" They are very respectful. That's why I think why she's a lot more open with these now.

FD: I'm not sure if you're aware of this, but in the last few years, there has really been a renaissance of all these special edition Blu-Ray of classic Hong Kong movies and it all started a few years ago with these boutique labels of the UK such as Eureka which this interview is for, 88 Films, Arrow; so they started doing all these deluxe special editions of classic Hong Kong film, Asian action film re-mastered with beautiful picture, beautiful audio and also with commentary tracks, bonus features, so they're almost like the criterion of Hong Kong action movie on Blu-Ray, so what's your opinion on this renaissance and popularity especially in the UK that lead to, again, people like us, or me, reaching out to your Mom to add some additional feature to her classic film which makes it look as good as it ever has?

TK: I think a lot of it has to do with folks our age and older. They are trying to, or a lot of it is the movie buffs, or the cinemaphiles where they're now seeing that, wow, this is a lost art form whether it is martial arts films or even Chow Yun Fat's films like the old cops and robbers, the Hong Kong style films right. The older like my Mom's martial art films, Bruce Lee martial art films and Sammo Hung all those guys; even Jackie Chan's early stuff, I think a lot of people are starting to see "We need to preserve this and we need to share this and let the younger generation know" so that they know that it didn't start with Michelle Yeoh or it didn't start with some of the new folks like Tony Jaa, so it started with these guys, these are the guys that started this.

FD: Your Mom even started before Bruce Lee.

TK: Well she started when she was like eighteen, seventeen.

FD: There is a famous interview where she said "When I was somebody, Jackie Chan was nobody". She joked of course

TK: Right, right, but Jackie was starting

FD: And a stuntman in a many of her films.

TK: He was just starting out when she was already famous. Not to disparage Jackie, he is amazing but we need to preserve that, I think that's the main thing. We need to show the younger generation that we didn't start with the folks you know now, it started back then. Even when Tony Leung was young, you know Tony Leung now because, well, he's Wenwu (in Shang-Chi), but have you seen him here!? When he did these roles and won the Asian equivalent of the Oscars, so that is what I kind of think it is. As you start to see the Asian representation in film, people start to look back, how did it start?

FD: Yeah I think a lot of people are doing that now.

TK: Yeah, I appreciate that, and also again, this is the fourth time now that I remember that I'm recollecting now is, wow! Yeah my Mom is that famous! She influenced the whole female martial arts genre.

FD: Yes, this renaissance lead to a magazine called "Eastern Heroes" that is a big deal and a big deal in Asian action cinema in the UK and after twenty years, they started to publish again.

TK: It's astounding what is happening and how it's happening. I'm appreciative of it as it keeps her legacy alive. If she is not here to tell the story it's hard as we're secondary. We don't know her life pre-us.

FD: Yes, I totally agree with you. It's about preserving Hong Kong cinema.

TK: It's a history. If we don't preserve it, especially Asian Americans or Asian Canadians or just Asians in general, if we don't preserve the history of this, it is going to be lost.

FD: Going back to the restaurant, any future plans for the "The Shack" or innovation or new plans?

TK: One of the things we thought about was how we bring this to folks that are not in this area which could be on-line ordering, in terms of how we ship it. So shipping readymade food you can cook at home. That's the new thing that's going on with "Fresh Meet", "Hello Fresh" all these guys. How do we do that from a local restaurant perspective? How do we get that out there? It's not just for "The Shack", it's for "Nan Bei Ho", the kind of thing of how do we get this out there, meaning, you're in Texas, you can't find this.

FD: Yeah like me, I'm in San Francisco and I can't eat the bean curd or the soy milk.

TK: Exactly! Like that. How do we get this out to everyone else? How do we make it so we're expanding virtually, not physically but virtually.

FD: Well, "Nan Bei Ho" is the established name and the standard of quality; I think "The Shack" is the place you need to check out. I think this place is pretty unique, it has great steak, great seafood and the atmosphere is fantastic. I just hope people come here and I hope all your fans that buy this Blu-Ray; please, when you come to New York, please take a trip to Queens.

TK: Come check us out. It is honestly where I hate to toot our own horn, but it's honestly where my brother my and I were confident that if you eat our food, you'll come straight back and you'll rave about it.

FD: I'll tell you a great story. Last time Bobby Samuels and I came here, he was all ready for "Nan Bei Ho" and last time we did the commentary for the Sammo Hung titles, he was all ready for "Nan Bei Ho" and like "Let's go see Angela, let's say hi". We went over to "Nan Bei Ho" and your Mom saw us and she was so surprised and pleased to see Bobby. She said "owww come, come, come" and dragged us away and we had no idea about this place, we had no idea, and we came here to "The Shack" and we sat down. Your brother, George, brought out the appetisers, the lobster mac, the lobster macaroni, the fried pickles and that wing, the soy garlic wings. We were like "Oh my God! This is so good!" and then I said "You know what, the next time we come back to New York, we gotta come back to "The Shack".

TK: Thank you. It's one of those things where we bill ourselves as comfort food. Somewhere where you can just come hang out and eat. Eat a main course and really just be yourself. You don't have to worry about who's sitting next to you, you can talk to them, we just really want it to be a family atmosphere.

五雷轟頂 THUNDERBOLT

監製 鄒文懷　茅瑛 田俊 白鷹 領銜主演　主演．李昆 陳菁 林蛟　導演：羅熾

五雷轟頂 THUNDERBOLT

FD: I look forward to coming back here each and every time I come back to New York, so thank you Thomas once again, say "Hi" to your Mom and good luck to you. I am really happy that we are able to preserve her legacy for the new generation.

TK: Thank you, I'm glad you're doing it as well, so thank you.

HECTOR MARTINEZ

SP: When did you first become aware of Angela Mao films and how did that come about?

HM: I was born in New York City in 1961 and was lucky enough to witness firsthand the "Kung Fu movie explosion" which started in 1973 with the first film released here being "5 Fingers of Death" aka "King Boxer." Then came "Lady Kung Fu" aka "Hapkido" and I instantly fell in love with Angela Mao.

SP: Which film ignited the fire with you for her films?

HM: "Lady Kung Fu" aka "Hapkido" which happened to be the first Kung Fu film starring a female heroine that we ever saw here in the U.S. Not only was she a supreme Martial Artist she also had this very calm and sweet demeanour, adding to the suspense of what she was capable of! Her characters have always had this "confidence" that was demonstrated by softness right before she was hard on her opponents, the perfect combination of Yin Yang!

SP: What made her standout to you over other martial artists at the time?

HM: I'd have to say her beauty and charm. Before Miss Mao I had never seen a woman with such beautiful and exotic looks take on a group of men in a fight and defeat them the way she did in her films!

SP: What are your top three films she made?

HM: "The Angry River" (her first and first film for Golden Harvest), "Deep Thrust" aka "Lady Whirlwind" and of course "Lady Kung Fu" aka "Hapkido".

SP: When was the first time you met her? Can you tell us about what it was like?

HM: I read a profile they did on Mrs. Mao in the New York Times Newspaper which covered her restaurant "Nan Bei Ho" which to my surprise and delight was located in Queens, NY. It was located a mere twenty minutes from my home.

I remember taking a trip there on a Saturday afternoon not knowing if she just "loaned" her name to the restaurant or if she would physically be there. The minute I walked in I saw her behind the counter attending her customers and immediately I turned and looked at my wife and said "There she is, Lady Whirlwind!" I stepped up to the counter and remember being a bit nervous (but much more excited) and I said "Hello Mrs. Mao" and in return she gave me the most pleasant smile. Right then and there I knew it was her, still beautiful and elegant after all these years.

SP: How has your relationship with Angela evolved over time?

HM: I really never thought about that but I can say that eating at her restaurant regularly with family and friends throughout the years has allowed me to enjoy her company as well as her family, they have come to know mine and her restaurant is like my second home. A lovely woman with a lovely family, I've been very blessed to have found her.

SP: Thomas King mentions that you were one of the reasons that Angela is more accepting of fans. You were very respectful. How does this make you feel?

HM: Again, I never knew that. All I can say is that growing up in church as well as my old school upbringing has taught me to show respect to my elders as well as to give them the space they deserve. Miss Mao is an icon, a legend in her field and therefore I treat her as such. But then again her hospitality and generosity is impeccable which makes it easier to respect her the more.

SP: Have you ever trained with Angela or seen her demonstrating? If so, can you tell us anything about that?

HM: No, I have never trained with Miss Mao but one time she did a Kung Fu move on me that was so fast that all I saw was a "flash!" She still has her moves and remains in remarkable shape and still looks incredibly youthful! She still is a "Deadly China Doll!"

SP: Whilst promoting the future of the martial arts industry, I believe we're at a point now where magazines, such as Eastern Heroes, have the responsibility to capture the culture and origins of martial arts cinema to preserve it for the future generations before it is lost. If someone that was not too familiar with Angela was reading this, and interested in learning, how would you describe Angela's legacy?

HM: I've always said that Angela Mao is the "female" Bruce Lee so that right there sums it up!

導演: 羅熾

主演: 李昆 陳菁 林蛟

嘉禾貢獻 最佳影片

轟頂 THUN

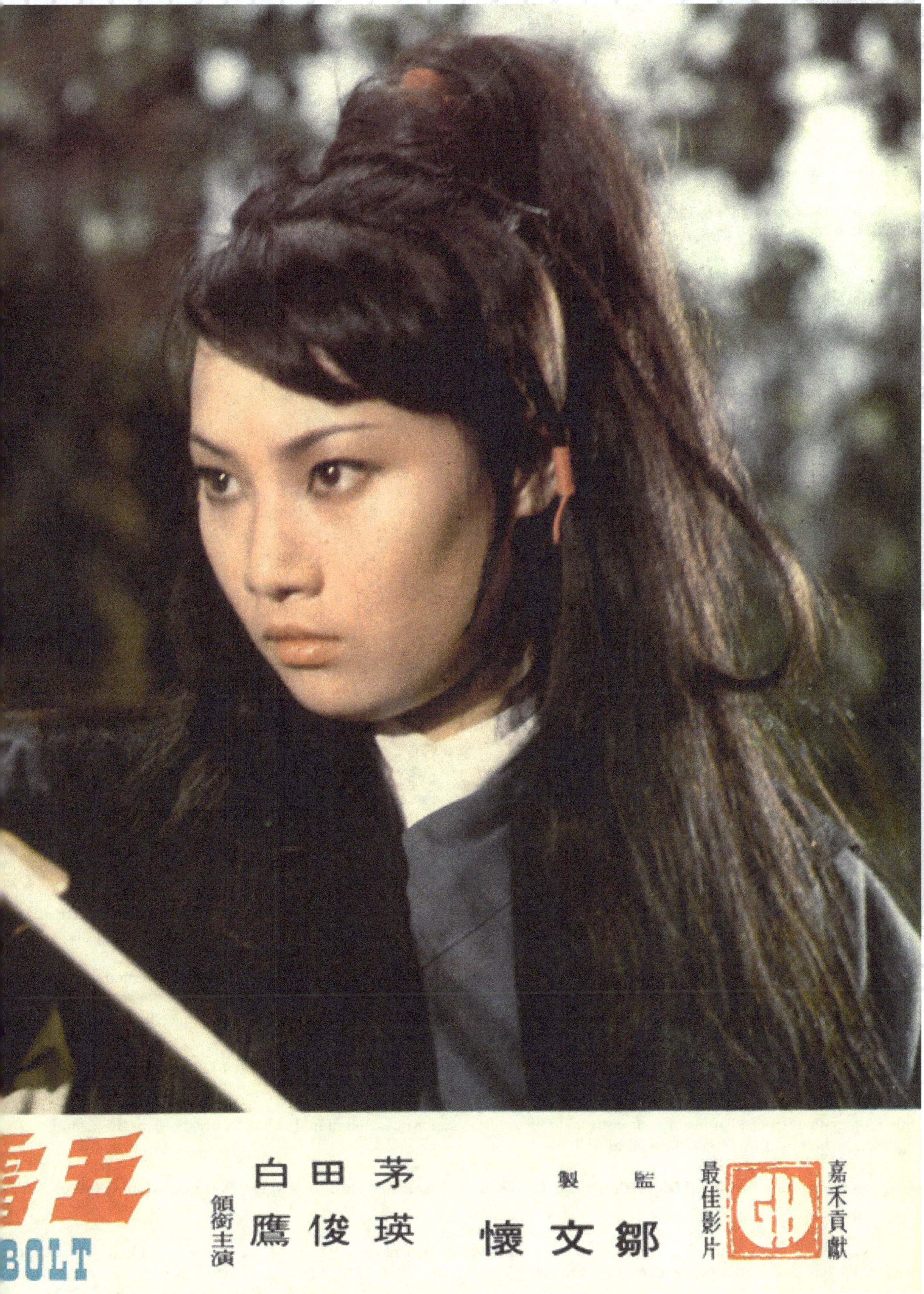

BOLT

茅 瑛　田 俊　白 鷹　領銜主演
監 製　鄒 文 懷
最佳影片　嘉禾貢獻

VINCENT LYN

SP: When did you first become aware of Angela Mao films and how did that come about?

VL: Like most teenagers during the Bruce Lee phenomenon, we would flock to see whatever movies we could get into. Growing up in London, many of these films were Rated X which was so ridiculous. So going to a cinema in Twickenham was when I saw the premiere of Hapkido in 1972 and was blown away. I like, so many young lads, fell in love with Angela immediately.

SP: What made her stand out to you over other martial artists at the time?

VL: Well here was this beautiful woman who could kickass. What more do you need than that? The first Queen of Kung Fu.

SP: What are your top three films she made?
VL: "Hapkido", "Enter the Dragon" and "When Taekwondo Strikes".

SP: When was the first time you met her? Can you tell us about it?

VL: I don't remember the year but it's about five years ago. A friend and Bruce Lee Collector, Hector Martinez, set up a get together at her restaurant in Queens, NY. Seeing her in person and how petite and dainty she was, but zipping around the restaurant as if she was twenty-five years old. It was wonderful to finally meet her.

SP: You arranged for Angela's Sifu, Master Ji Han Jae to surprise her at the New York ceremony. What do you remember about this? Angela must have been very happy?

VL: Yes, Master Ji Han Jae met his student Angela Mao after more than thirty years. Although they live in neighboring states, New Jersey & New York, and they never knew it! Angela was stunned! it was priceless to see the genuine caring and love for each other. Beautiful. She was constantly looking after him holding his hand like an old father. Such respect and admiration.

SP: How did it come about you and your father introduced Angela to Her Majesty Queen of the Democratic Republic of Congo?

VL: Her Majesty Queen Diambi Kabatusuila of Congo was part of United Nations delegates that was brought to Angela's restaurant for a celebration dinner.
I think most people were shocked knowing that actual royalty was with us. But more so that Queen Diambi was so such a cool and down to earth person.

SP: How has your friendship with Angela developed over time?

VL: Our friendship is of mutual respect. For me of course she laid the groundwork for my generation to follow in her footsteps. It's a family and I'm also happy to have become friends with her sons as well.

SP: Lastly, thank you very much for speaking with us and do you have any stories about Angela that you wish to tell us about?

VL: Angela will always be the Queen of Kung Fu. There are countless stories and many of us could write books on her. But I know we are all better off knowing that she has touched our hearts all over the world.

ROBERT SAMUELS

SP: When did you first become aware of Angela Mao films and how did it come about?

RS: Growing up I was a big fan of the Shaw Brothers. Chang Cheh & Lau Chia Laing were my favourite team at the time. However when Raymond Chow branched out and formed Golden Harvest.

That's when I started paying attention to the style of filmmaking from Golden Harvest. That's when I first took notice of Angela Mao. Up until then it was mostly about male brotherhood that Chang Cheh had first introduced to the audiences. Outside of Chang Pei Pei, Angela Mao was different. She exuded the same heroic vibe that the male action stars were exhibiting at the time only she was beautiful and deadly at the same time.

SP: Which film ignited the fire with you for her films?

RS: Well that's easy! "Sting of the Dragon" aka: "When Taekwondo Strikes" was the first time I saw her in a film; with Jhoon Rhee and my Sifu Sammo Hung. Then "Hapkido" followed by Thunderbolt (1970), The Invincible Eight (1971), Deadly China Doll (1972) etc. The fierce way she fights was just as powerful as the male leads at Golden Harvest Studios. Of course her scene in Enter the Dragon is probably the most powerful

emotional scene in the Film.

SP: What made her standout to you over other martial artists at the time?

RS: Female Action stars at the time were far and wide most came from Shaw Brothers. She was the first breakout star at Golden Harvest when I was growing up. She had a certain swag with how she carried her performances. It didn't hurt that she was incredibly beautiful also.

SP: What are your top three films she made?

RS: I would have to say my top three films for me are "Hapkido", "When Taekwondo Strikes", and "Thunderbolt". These are my personal favourites because she showed so much skill and acting in these films which made them instant classics. She could handle the choreography as well as the male actors.

SP: When was the first time you met her? Can you tell us about it?

RS: The first time was when my friend and Brother Alex Richter and his family asked me to go to her restaurant to grab a meal and meet her. We had heard she lived in Queens N.Y and had a successful restaurant.

When we arrived the Queen herself was there and her son. We started talking about the golden age of Hong Kong cinema and I shared with her the fact that Sammo Hung was my Sifu. Angela immediately brightened up saying Sammo was her big brother and that she had so much love and respect for him. That night it all changed for me she treated us as family from that moment forward. I owe Alex a debt of gratitude.

SP: Have you ever trained with Angela or seen her demonstrating? If so, can you tell us anything about that?

RS: No, I never trained with her .She has pretty much retired and her family is her number one priority. Although when we were talking about some of the films she worked on she got a bit animated describing some of the action, that's when I got a glimpse into what she was like as a screen fighter.

SP: Angela has worked with Sammo Hung in a lot of her classic films, how did she react to knowing you were a personal student of his and even his bodyguard?

RS: From the very first time when she found out, it was like she put me in a different category. Then about several months later I bought another one of her friends to see her, Shaw Brothers Veteran Lu Feng. They knew each other very well. They grew up together in Taiwan. Their families know each other and that was so special for her to see him after so many years.

After that day she said Sammo Hung was her big brother and that anytime I wanted to come and visit I was welcome. I had the opportunity to meet her husband and two sons all of whom are just the kindest people on Earth.

SP: One important question, martial arts aside, I've heard about "The Shack". The steaks, the chicken..... What's it like? How do they cook the meat? What kind of flavours are going on?

RS: Hell yes! "The SHACK", that is her second restaurant she recently opened with her sons. The cuisine is American and Seafood. I've never had a steak like that and garlic wings, lobster, mac & cheese, just so much creative meals. If you're ever in the Queens N.Y. area I would definitely recommend stopping by and grabbing a meal.

SP: Lastly, thank you very much for speaking with us and do you have any stories about Angela that you wish to tell us about?

RS: I told her that she helped give me inspiration and believe that I could achieve anything. We talked about our love for Sammo and how much he has done for us. She loves him dearly. She refuses to seek the limelight in anyway. However, she did come out once to honour Sammo Hung at the New York Asian Film Festival where he received a Lifetime Achievement Award.

She really enjoyed seeing him and presenting him that distinguished honour. I remember one conversation we had about her career and how she feels about the industry now. I told her "Sometimes we can choose to make history, and sometimes history chooses us". She is an icon among fans of Hong Kong Cinema. People will always come to just see her and say "hi", that comes with history choosing us.

SP: When did you first become aware of Angela Mao films and how did that come about?

AR: The first time I saw Angela Mao in a film was in "Enter the Dragon" when I was eight years old. I didn't know who she was, but I remember being very impressed with her movements and thinking that she really did seem like she was skilful enough to be the sister to Bruce Lee's character.

ALEX RICHTER

SP: Which film ignited the fire with you for her films?

AR: Beyond my initial introduction to Angela through "Enter the Dragon", I think the second movie I saw her in was "Stoner" opposite George Lazenby. I was a teenager when I saw that film and I recall watching it mostly because I thought the title was funny and because it starred the "one and done" Bond. But it wasn't until I saw her in "Hapkido" when I realized that she was a bona fide star in her own right. "Hapkido" is a fantastic introduction to what Angela can do.

SP: What made her standout to you over other martial artists at the time?

AR: Angela stood out not only because she was skilful in her own right, but she was also able to hold her own with the giants of the industry. She was able to look believable when she fought because of her movement and power. Her acting was on point and her character always fought in a way that matched the role she was playing.

SP: What are your top three films she made?

AR: I'm a big fan of the film "The Tournament", a film where she squares off with Sammo Hung. That movie is criminally underrated in my opinion. My other two favourites are "When Taekwondo Strikes" and "Broken Oath".

SP: When was the first time you met Angela? Can you tell us about it?

AR: I'm not sure if it was the first or second time I met her, but I remember coming to her restaurant with my good friend, Sammo Hung protégé Bobby Samuels. As soon as we got to the restaurant Bobby had to use the restroom. I told Angela in Cantonese that "Sammo Hung's student" was there with me and he would be out to see her in a moment. I assume she thought that Sammo Hung's student would be Chinese. When she finally saw Bobby, she seemed surprised that he was "not Chinese" yet spoke Cantonese. The three of us spoke in Cantonese and I can imagine it was an interesting moment for her.

SP: Have you ever trained with Angela or seen her demonstrating? If so, can you tell us anything about that?

AR: No, I have not, but she did watch me do a Wing Tsun demonstration once. I've given demos in front of Kung Fu masters in Hong Kong, but I don't think I was ever more nervous than when I demonstrated in front of Angela!

SP: I have heard stories that Angela may have had plans in regard to a film with Bruce Lee before Bruce passed. Do you know whether there is any truth in that?

AR: I don't know any specific stories, but it goes to reason that if Bruce would have made any more films in Hong Kong, then he would have definitely made a film with Angela at some point.

SP: Lastly, thank you very much for speaking with us and do you have any stories about Angela that you wish to tell us about?
AR: The best moment I have with Angela must have been the time we brought her co-star and Hapkido teacher Ji Han Jae to her restaurant. Of course, most people know Ji Han Jae from his fight scene with Bruce Lee in the unfinished "Game of Death".

Angela starred with him in the film "Hapkido", but their relationship was more than that, he was also her teacher in "Hapkido". He was so impressed with her skills that I believe he awarded her the 2nd or 3rd Dan black belt in the art.

In a weird twist of fate both Ji Han Jae and Angela emigrated to the US a long time ago yet had no idea. For year Ji Han Jae lived not too far away from Angela, yet they had not seen each other since 1972. It was a long-awaited reunion!
Angela was nearly in tears when she saw him and she took care of him just a student would their teacher. As Angela does not speak much English I served as the translator. It was an honour to translate for both and I had to pinch myself that it was really happening. I was eating food and translating conversation with two stars that I watched in films since I was a child! I will never forget that.

FRANK DJENG

SP: When did you first become aware of Angela Mao films and how did that come about?

FD: I became aware of her films after I was asked to be her interpreter at the 2010 New York Asian Film Festival where she was presenting Sammo Hung with the Lifetime Achievement Award. At that time I only knew her from" Enter The Dragon" and because the films that she made in her prime were hardly available on video (or in very poor condition) that I've never seen a single one of them.

It's only when I was invited to the ceremony and upon reading her bios and talking to those who were at the event that I realised she has such a large body of work that I have hardly seen.

SP: Which film ignited the fire with you for her films?

FD: Definitely "Hapkido". She was amazing in it, especially once she unleashes her fury during the last thirty minutes of the film.

SP: What made her standout to you over other martial artists at the time?

FD: How cold and furious she was, especially her gaze, and how elegant she moves. To call her the female Bruce Lee was most appropriate.

SP: What are your top three films she made?

FD: "Hapkido", "Broken Oath", and "When Taekwondo Strikes", with an honorary mention to "Lady Whirlwind". I just like how "Western" that film was, with a great and unexpected ending.

SP: When was the first time you met her? Can you tell us about it?

FD: I first met her at the 2010 NYAFF like I mentioned before but I had almost no communication with her because I wasn't backstage, so when I was ready to do the interpretation for her I just went up to the stage from the theatre, where I was standing.
It was a wonderful experience interpreting for her as she's charming, funny and very humble. And I never saw her again after the ceremony; she was whisked away and I left for dinner! It's only until I started working on my documentary on Bruceploitation films that I got in touch with her son, George, and arranged an interview with her in March of 2017 and that's when I really started to get to know her. She was most gracious in her interview and couldn't be more kind.

SP: How has your relationship with Angela evolved over time?

FD: I think that, now that I've met her several times, interviewed her twice, and went to both her restaurant and her son's restaurant many times (I would go eat there every time I go to New York), I think she's realised that I wasn't there just to interview her or get a picture taken. I genuinely care about her legacy and I want to do all I can to promote her restaurants because the food is really, really good, and as a foodie I know good food when I eat it, so by 2022, twelve years since I first met her, I consider her a friend and not just a celebrity that I happen to know

CYNTHIA ROTHROCK

SP: When did you first become aware of Angela Mao films and how did that come about?

CR: The first time I saw Angela Mao was in "Enter the Dragon". I was a beginner in martial arts at that time. At that time there were not a lot of girls studying Martial Arts so I was so happy to see a woman fight.

SP: Which film ignited the fire with you for her films?

CR: "Enter the Dragon" because that was the first one I saw her in.

SP: What made her standout to you over other martial artists at the time?

CR: I never saw a strong female fighting in film for the first time. I was so impressed to see this because at this time martial arts in America were considered a male sport by the majority of people. To see a female fight like the men and still hold her grace and femininity was a role model for me.

SP: What are your top three films she made?

CR: "Enter the Dragon", "Hapkido" and "Deadly China Doll"

SP: As a Grandmaster in Tang Soo Do, Angela's style also has Korean influences with the locks and takedowns etc. which of her films impress you?

CR: My styles are Korean and Chinese and when I do my films I combine both styles... I think I related to Angela because she did the same combining both styles of fighting in her films.

SP: When you were working for Golden Harvest in Hong Kong; you had a crazy time with filming and flying back to the USA for competitions, did you ever get any spare time in Hong Kong?

CR: Yes, there was a lot of time to socialize. My first film "Yes Madam" took almost eight months to shoot. We did not shoot every day. I learned mahjong, and drinking games quite well.

SP: Last year (2021) "New York Ninja" was finally released. You filmed this in 1984 with Don "The Dragon" Wilson and

John Barryman (Pluto from Hills Have Eyes). This film has a rating of 96% on Rotten Tomatoes and has sat in a warehouse for nearly forty years before "Vinegar Syndrome" released it on Blu-Ray. It is already a collector item and selling for double the RRP. What do you remember about this film?

CR: This is a very interesting story. Don Wilson and I were not in "New York Ninja" as actors. We only did the voices for "Vinegar Syndrome". Vinegar Syndrome found the footage, no sound, no script and could not get in touch with the real actors except one. So they made a script to what they thought the actors were saying and we had to go in and sync it to their lips. I thought that the movie was so bad, that it came out as a brilliant comedy. When I went to the screening I loved it... it was very funny, but perhaps in parts that were not meant to be funny. Surely and entertainment piece of work.

SP: Do you have any films planned for the future?

CR: Yes, I have quite a few upcoming, "Wrath of Prey" which is completed, about to shoot "No Time to Die", and reuniting with my friend Alexander Nevsky on another film, and I'm currently shooting "Black Belt Theater" for Jungo Plus.

SP: Lastly, thank you very much for speaking with us and do you have any last words for Angela?

CR: I have never met Angela, but I am inspired for all that she has accomplished. I have followed the same path and very much hope to meet her in the future.

RICK BAKER

SP: When did you first become aware of Angela Mao films and how did that come about?

RB: My first introduction to Angela was way back in 1974 when I saw "Enter the Dragon" at my local cinema. At that time with the exception of Bruce Lee, I had little knowledge of any of the other cast members.

On the way out I purchased a copy of "Bruce Lee Exciting Cinema Kung Fu magazine" in 1974 which I still have. Flicking through the pages it highlighted members of the cast in particular an advert for the coming release of "Hapkido" starring Angela Mao. Her small but important role in the movie had made an impact on me like several others of the cast including Bolo and Jim Kelly. But as a fourteen year old watching a beautiful fighting femme fatal had me wanting to see more of her in action and so my journey began into the world of Hong Kong Cinema.

SP: Which film ignited the fire with you for her films?

RB: At that time, there were very few films available to see this tiny powerhouse of fury in! Accept those that had been packaged in by Golden Harvest on the back of Bruce lee's success. But still to this day "Hapkido" and "When "Taekwondo Strikes" both got a theatrical releases back then and they still rank in my favourite movies that Angela starred in. Of course over the years, I have managed to see most of her movies and I would add to that list "The Fate of Lee Khan", "The Himalayan" and "Broken Oath".

SP: What made her standout to you over other martial artists at the time?

RB: Angela definitely had a screen presence that won her many adoring fans, with a mixture of beauty and martial arts skills. Seeing a petite lady going to fist to fingernail with a variety of opponents made for exciting cinema. Also, in the UK more females were inspired after seeing her to take up martial arts back in the 70s and she quickly became an icon thus given the name "The Queen of Kung Fu".

SP: What are your top three films she made?

RB: "Hapkido"

As I mentioned in the previous question, having seen most of her movies now so the choice is vast. I will always put "Hapkido" as my favourite remembering the fond memories of getting into see the movie on three occasions under age. While not the first film to depict such a situation, the Angela Mao-led, Huang Feng-directed "Hapkido" This is certainly one of the more enjoyable Angela Mao-led movies, directed by Huang Feng. Set in the early 1930s, when Japan occupied Korea. "Hapkido" is packed with great action scenes, combined with a stellar period setting and a story that makes this one of the best Golden Harvest Movies of that time.
"When Taekwondo Strikes"

Although Angela Mao is the main draw card here, she doesn't appear until twenty minutes into the movie. But it is such a welcome sight as she starts to kick and chop her way in, sending those Japanese flying through thin walls and breaking almost everything while doing it. She has a wonderful screen presence and excels in both her acting and fighting Skills. In "The Angry River", she only fights with a sword; however, it's a blast to see her letting loose here with her real, bare hands, Taekwondo style.

"Broken Oath" is a real triumph of Hong Kong filmmaking, showing off what a cast and crew full of HK's finest could do in the late 70s. It's got some fine acting from Angela Mao, some superb kicking from Bruce Leung, and enough plot twists and colourful characters to keep the audience interested. It doesn't have Lady Snow blood's stunning visuals and blood-spattered extras, but it more than makes up for it with sheer kinetic ferocity.

SP: 'With all the jobs in all the world', how did you originally get into martial arts films and decide to dedicate a career to promoting the culture, films, stars?

RB: Truthfully, I saw "King Boxer" my very first Kung Fu movie in 1974, just prior to seeing the "Big Boss". I already had a fascination with Bruce Lee from just seeing clips on TV and reading about his untimely death in a newspaper article the day after he died.

I remember writing my first item in Kung Fu monthly poster magazine around 1976 in the letters page. Despite being hooked and practicing martial arts, by the time I was 18 I had discovered girls and nightclubs derailing me from my passion. It was not until 1988, when I went to the Chinese late night movies that "Eastern Condors" was playing and I was hooked again! Which in turn, this inspired me to change the "UK Jackie Chan Fan Club" and re name it to the now familiar brand name "Eastern Heroes" and create my own magazine and start to do triple bill film screenings at The Scala, Kings Cross London.

From small acorns we grew, and we started to approach guests to come over to the UK. Having raised our profile with are bestselling book "The Essential Guide to Hong Kong movies" we found our credibility made it far more possible to convince guests to come over and greet their fans. We then created our own video label and started to distribute the smaller independent Kung Fu movies. Finally we managed to create our own TV show with Jonathon Ross it's been an interesting journey.

SP: Through all the changes in media formats, even from physical to digital, how did you keep the Eastern spirit alive in the UK and financially viable, from the 1980's until now, in such constantly changing environment?

RB: It's been difficult and I have been through many lows. There is a saying "It's not the strong that will survive, it's those that can adapt".

This is how I have managed to keep the name and magazine going despite taking a break for a few years. I count my blessings that I have managed to make my passion my work and hope to continue well into retirement age.

SP: As Thomas King mentioned, you have revised the Eastern Heroes magazine recently, what made you take the leap back into magazines?

RB: I have to say it was the lockdown of Covid 19 that saw me at home wondering what to do; this became the "Eureka" moment to see if there would be any response to me re-launching Eastern Heroes.

We had tried before in 2014, but it did not get the response I had hoped for, so I had to re-evaluate how people would respond seven years later in 2021. With online publishing available and distribution offered on line by Amazon and Barnes & Noble, it felt I could reach a new audience. Also shipping from the UK can put people off with the inflated postage charges, but now people can order from around the world and get free shipping.

Collectors often prefer physical media as opposed to e-magazines. So far the results have proved better than my expectations and hope to see the magazine keep growing over the next few years.

SP: The UK is now leading in the boutique Blu-Ray and 4k Ultra discs for Martial Arts. Companies such as Eureka Entertainment, Arrow and 88 films have been re-mastering and coming out all sorts of awesome special features discs and posters etc. Do you think this sudden eruption in Eastern films in the UK has any longevity?

RB: I think it can last whilst there are good classic titles and good extras there is an audience. The standard of these releases have been superb and the restorations have made the films much more watchable reaching new audiences that where not even born when most of these titles were released. Golden Harvest and Shaw Brothers have a healthy back catalogue of great Kung Fu movies so I think we these release are safe for a few more years

SP: Thank you for the time Boss, lastly, do you have any words for Angela?

RB: I would have loved her to come to the UK for an event, to let her see how her popularity is still very much alive due to the release I just spoke of in the last question. If she wants to come I will make it happen.

FILMOGRAPHY

Angela has starred in 38 films during her career 1970 to 1992 listed below.

The Angry River (1970) – Lan Feng
Thunderbolt (1970)
The Invincible Eight (1971)
Deadly China Doll (1972) – Hei Lu
Hapkido (1972) – Yu Ying
Lady Whirlwind (1972) – Miss Tien
Enter the Dragon (1973) – Su Lin
Back Alley Princess (1973) – Ying
When Taekwondo Strikes (1973) – Wan Ling-Ching
The Two Great Cavaliers (1973)
The Fate of Lee Khan (1973)
Naughty! Naughty! (1974)
Stoner (1974) – Angela Li Shou-Hua
The Invincible Kung Fu Trio (1974)
The Tournament (1974)
The Himalayan (1975)
International Assassins (1976) – Queen of Cambodia
Lady Karate (1976)
Duel with the Devils (1977) – Chu
Invincible (1976)
A Queen's Ransom (1976)
The Eternal Conflict (1976) – Fei Fei
Duels in the Desert (1977)
Broken Oath (1977) – Lotus Lin
The Damned (1978)
Iron Maiden (1978) – Chin Lun
Scorching Sun, Fierce Wind, Wild Fire (1978)
Return of the Tiger (1978)
Dance of Death (1979)
Snake Deadly Act (1979) – Brothel Madam
Flying Masters of Kung Fu (1979)
Moonlight Sword and Jade Lion (1981)
The Stunning Gambling (1982)
Ninja, the Violent Sorcerer (1982) – Anna (uncredited)
Book and Sword Chronicles (TV series) (1984) – Luo Bing
Eastern Condors (1987) (extra)
Devil Dynamite (1987)
Ghost Bride (1992)

Source - https://en.wikipedia.org/wiki/Angela_Mao#Filmography

CONTRIBUTORS

A dedication to the people that made this happen; for whom I am eternally grateful.

Hector Martinez
- Martial Art movie expert
- Bruce Lee specialist
- Specialist collector
- Eastern Heroes contributor
- Martial Arts expert on the "Bruce Lee Channel"

Vincent Lyn
- CEO/Founder at We Can Save Children
- International Human Rights Commission Director of Creative Development at African Views Organization
- Economic & Social Council at United Nations
- Editor in Chief & Middle East Correspondent at Wall Street News Agency
- Rescue & Recovery Specialist at International Confederation of Police & Security Experts

Robert Samuels
- Actor
- Action Movie Star
- Stunt coordinator
- Action director
- 2nd unit director
- Hung Gar Kung Fu Master
- Inductee into the Hong Kong Stuntman's Association
- Founder of the first Western stunt team in Hong Kong.

Alex Richter
- Chief Instructor of City Wing Tsun
- Author
- YouTuber
- Podcaster
- TV Martial Arts expert (VICE, The Discovery Channel, NBC, PBS and more)
- Eight Level Master by the Wushu Kung Fu Masters Association (Hong Kong)
- Certified in K3 Combat Movement Systems under Dr. Mark Cheng and Dr. Jimmy Yuan

James Chu
- James Chu spent his youngest years in Hong Kong when martial arts films were getting recognition both in Hong Kong and overseas.
- James grew up with movies and spent more time in cinemas when he was young watching Bruce Lee, Sammo Hung, Jackie Chan and Chow Yun Fat.
- James has maintained a keen interest in action movies from Hong Kong and Asia after coming to the UK in the 1980s.
- James is particularly interested in how martial arts films have evolved over the years and how that reflects the Chinese cultural identity.

Caleb Hui
- Caleb is currently studying in Oxford in UK.
- Caleb has been fascinated by martial arts since he started watching films.
- Caleb started practicing Chinese Martial Arts since he was a child for nearly a decade now.
- Caleb has won multiple awards in different competitions including being a regional champion of the Greater Bay area of China in 2019.
- Caleb hopes that in translating and transcribing this interview; those valuable words will be spread to an even wider audience.

Cynthia Rothrock
- Actor
- Action Movie Star
- Co-Host of "Black Belt Theater"
- 8th Degree in Tang Soo Do
- 5-Time Undefeated World Champion
- Author
- Black Belt Hall of Fame Inductee
- Owner of Cynthia Rothrock Martial Arts Association
- https://association.cynthiarothrockofficial.com/

Johnny Burnett & Zhijun Liu
- YouTuber
- YouTube.com/thefanaticaldragon
- Eastern Heroes contributors
- Martial Arts movie expert
- Translator

Ricky Baker
- Owner of Eastern Heroes Magazine
- Editor
- International memorabilia seller at www.Easternheroes.com
- Publisher of Bruce Lee special magazine
- TV Presenter/ creator "Stop Kung Fu!"
- Author of "The Essential Guide to Hong Kong Movies" & "Essential Guide to Deadly China Dolls"
- Video distributer
- Film festival organiser bringing many A-List stars to the UK; Chow Yun Fat, Jet Li, John Woo, Donnie Yen, Maggie Cheung, Hwang Jung Li, Cynthia Rothrock, Gordon Lui, Charng Shan and more!
- Currently developing several movie projects

親愛的茅女士：

謝謝妳抽空接受我們的訪問。能參與製作今次的訪問，我深感榮幸。我希望妳喜歡我們製作的成果，並能在訪問中勾起妳一些美麗的回憶。送上我們對妳的尊敬，並祝妳一切平安！Simon Pritchard 敬上

每次見到您並與您交談總是很高興。非常感謝您從百忙之中抽出時間讓我採訪您。我期待下次回到紐約時再次見到您並享用您餐廳的美味佳餚。祝 安好 Frank Djeng 敬

Final thoughts - Frank Djeng

To tell you a bit about myself, I have been nicknamed "The Master of Remaster" although I now prefer "The Commentary Maestro".

I have been busy with recording audio commentaries for all the classic Hong Kong cinema titles, including the UK boutique labels, like Eureka, 88 Films, and Arrow.

I am recording over thirty commentaries for 2022 alone. My upcoming projects include "Running Out of Time 1 and 2" and four other Johnnie To titles, "Jackie Chan's Police Story trilogy", Michelle Yeoh classics, Yuen Biao gems, "On The Run", "The Ice Man Cometh" and "Righting Wrongs" which also stars Cynthia Rothrock. I have also been working on the early Zhang Yimou gem "The Road Home" with Zhang Ziyi.

I have heard that the UK fans are super excited for the "Jackie Chan's Police Story trilogy" and have been waiting for a long, long time for a Blu-Ray remaster of "The Iceman Cometh". I hope we do these justice and the fans enjoy them.

Simon Pritchard

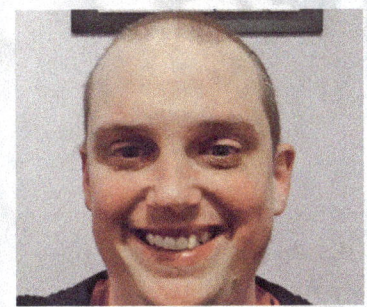

What a rollercoaster this has been…. 'The blood, the sweat, the beers!'

I hope this gives you a real insight into one of the original stars, and a true legend from the golden age of Kung Fu cinema, Angela Mao.

Finally, I would like to especially thank the following people:

- Frank: For working with me to create this and all the invaluable help and advice along the way. This article would not have evolved into anything like this without you.
- James: For reaching out, the dedication & professionalism in translating Angela's interview.
- Caleb: For the time it must have taken to do the actual transcription whilst translating Angela's interview. It was done to very high standard and we were impressed. When you finish your education and pass your gradings; you definitely have a bright future ahead.
- Meg: "Momma" Pritchard (Bachelor of Education (Hons), RSA Qualified Typist) for proofreading and constant support.
- Rick: For having the faith in me, continuous advice, support and making things happen for real!

ANGELA MAO
The Poster Princess
By Alan Donkin

Angela Mao starred in some of the best kung fu films of the 1970s. Many of the posters for these films are much sought-after by collectors for various reasons. Some fans collect the memorabilia of their favourite movies. Others just like the artwork. Whatever the motives, Angela Mao appears on some of the finest posters of the decade.

This article is a rundown of her best theatrical posters. No gimmicks this time. It's just my favourites, in order, homers only. Sadly, it meant I had to miss out the incredible Korean variant of Proud Horses in the Flying Sand (1977), which would easily have made the top ten. I had to draw the line somewhere, though. There are dozens of Thai versions, for example, but it would take an entire magazine to include them.

22. A Queens Ransom (1976)

Jimmy Wang Yu, George Lazenby and Angela star in this Raymond Chow-produced movie, which is advertised by a theatrical poster that I'd describe as 'ok'. I get all the best lines from Jared King. There's nothing wrong with the design – there's just nothing particularly attention-grabbing either.

21. Moonlight Sword and Jade Lion (1977)

The black backdrop is effective, the red text is nicely bordered by yellow, and the inclusion of a fight scene is welcome. However, the character images are a tad cluttered, and the great big lump of jade taking up half the poster is a bit too garish for me.

20. The Association (1975)

The green background is lovely, and the imagery isn't too busy. The target on Byong Yu looks great, providing the audience with a sneak peek at the theme of the film. Angela adopts a fighting pose, wholly different to the other female cast members shown. A decent poster, but not particularly memorable.

19. The Tournament (1974)

Everything about this poster should work for me. It should be elite level. It's hand-drawn, full of action and contains some great snippets from the film. I just can't like it as much as I ought to. The blood splash feels overly-fussy, and the green font doesn't sit well alongside it. Angela's image – the centrepiece of the whole thing – looks slightly dislocated below the knee on the kicking leg. I don't know if it's a perspective issue, but the whole stance doesn't present enough power. Even the sky-blue English text clashes.

18. Bandits, Prostitutes and Silver (1977)

Gold backgrounds rarely work, and this is no exception! It's a shame, because everything else is competently arranged. The flowerhead of characters in the centre features iconic stars of the 70s, and the horsemen spread across the page behind them is neat. Again, Angela is shown fighting, in arguably the most badass, toughest stance of the ensemble, which shows the esteem that her abilities were held in. Her martial arts ability was a huge draw, and producers knew it.

17. The Legendary Strike (1978)

What have we got here? A gorgeously blended backdrop of yellow and orange, with red text splashed diagonally across it. Numerous fighting stances struck by Chen Sing, Carter Wong, et al. But who towers above them in an elegant crane style? Angela Mao – and she looks great on this poster. The very epitome of grace and class.

16. When Taekwondo Strikes (1973)

I haven't got this poster, but I wish I did. It's a nightmare to find. And for good reason! It's a great little effort, that I'm convinced will look more effective in real life than it does on a small photo. There's a flurry of kicks beneath Angela, stacking up the content of the film nicely, but her punch sets her apart from the rest. The red backdrop lacks subtlety, but it's a well-balanced arrangement that puts our star at the top of the tree.

15. Two Great Cavaliers (1978)

Another one that's rarer than an original idiom. I know the photographic montage posters have their detractors, but shush. This poster is great! The symmetry of the action in the top half of the design is massively satisfying, and the natural blue sky backdrop is exquisite. Even the font colours fit together well. The film has a terrific cast – John Liu, Chen Sing and Leung Kar-Yan are the main players – but who is at the front of them all? Never be in doubt that Angela Mao was a superstar who put bums on seats.

14. Lady Whirlwind (1972)

This is a great design. Chang Yi is superbly sketched, and the ghostly Pai Ying figure at the bottom emerges from the swirling whirlpool of blues and whites very effectively. You can even see the brush strokes in that background. Beautiful. Angela is nicely drawn in a 'just about to launch into a cartwheel' way. There are two reasons why this doesn't rank higher in the list. First, the leg-blur effect. I don't like it. It's such a fake way of generating energy in an image. Second, the text. It's as subtle as a spade to the face. With the blade held sideways. It's just too brash, and detracts from the wonderful artwork.

13. Back Alley Princess (1973)

This is more of a Polly Shang-Kuan flick, but I have to include it! Angela has fourth billing, ok? The incredible Golden Harvest style once again shines through, with the two fighters trading blows in the top half. See - you don't need multiple image blur to generate raw, kinetic energy in a hand-drawn fight scene! The text is presented in the style of a late 1960s Shaw Brothers poster, with deep 3D blocks for each character. I'm not sure that the black and white pyramid of faces works. It just seems plonked on top of everything else. Great poster, though.

12. Snake Deadly Act (1979) – first variant

Ah. HYPOCRITE ALERT. Yeah, ahem, well I can worm my way out of this one. I think. I'll address the elephant in the room first. The hand blur looks terrible, and is the weakest part of the poster by far. Get rid of that nonsense and it's a near-perfect design. What I like about this poster is the painting style. Fung Hak-On's image is created using bold, meaty strokes, and deep, rich colours. The little photo battles taking place around Angela are great. It's not the type of design I've seen before, and I appreciate the way the painted elements take centre stage. The black font with its yellow border is lovely, and even the English text has been cracked down the middle.

11. Stoner (1974)

Another George Lazenby flick. Angela gets equal prominence in this stunning poster, which benefits from real study. There's so many design aspects that the artist has nailed. The sunset backdrop is dream-like, providing an unobtrusive framing for all the foreground elements. The two leads are drawn with a real eye for character. All the shenanigans below are tasteful rather than sleazy, and the entire poster is bordered with thick wooden lines. Something that really works is the way the background never reaches the border – white paint has been applied to keep them separate. It's a very smooth effect. The text is written in subtle fonts that don't clash, and even the English text at the top is presented inside a stylish plaque.

10. Hapkido (1972)

Where do I start with this gem? Everything – every single thing – is beautifully sketched. Notice the way that each character has different levels of clarity? Angela is perhaps the most clearly rendered. The figure in the bottom right is so vague, it's like he was drawn using oil pastels. The colouring is exquisite – the two 'main' images are presented in lifelike tones, whereas the other two are created using riffs of a single colour. The image at the top of the page is absolutely superb – even the fist above Angela's head is fantastic. A poster of genuine class. Note: This photo is from Ray Farrell's collection, so it features the added bonus of a Whang In-Shik autograph at the bottom.

9. Revenge of Kung Fu Mao (1977)

I sense a credibility nosedive coming on. Put the knives away for now and give me a chance! This poster is excellent. It's all photos, granted, but as a collage of stars and action, I can't see much wrong with it. The background is really bold and adventurous – the transition from red to sky blue, through brown, maroon and violet – is a brave one that totally works. The cast photos are presented in tidy little circles. Every cast member has their name beside them. It just looks classy. Wong Tao looks badass (as Johnny Lawrence might say), and Angela takes pride of place in the centre of the poster, holding a wooden seat in a combat stance! Come on! It looks bloody fantastic! I haven't even mentioned the equine epicness at the foot of the page. If you have this poster and don't like it, then sell it to me, please, because I love it!

8. Snake Deadly Act (1979)
second variant

Hello? Police? Yeah, I want to report a crime. A most serious and regrettable one. What is it? Oh, it's pretty simple. It is a crime that this poster isn't more well-known and that I don't have it in my collection. Hypocrisy reigns supreme, again, for we have an embarrassment of motion blur going on here. I'll hear none of it, though. Apart from that obvious flaw, the rest of the poster is a triumph. No photos this time, just sublimely painted characters in a variety of poses and action shots. A couple of them even have their own little box-outs, with individualised backdrop colours. The general background design and colours are amazing. The circles seem to contain everything AND allow the images to burst out of them. The fonts look great against the darkness, too. This is a special, special poster.

7. Scorching Sun, Fierce Winds, Wild Fire (1977)

This design is a bit of a throwback to the early 1970s stuff. Everything is hand-drawn, and hand-drawn well. The amazing line-up (Tien Peng, Chang Yi, Tan Tao-Liang, Lo Lieh and Angela Mao) deserve something special, and this poster provides it. The cast bursting from the sun is really classy, and the red background ties in nicely with the fire mentioned in the title. The fierce winds seem to be associated with the horses at the bottom of the page – they're eye-openingly well-sketched as they frantically plough through the white trails that artists use to denote wind. The single Achilles heel of this poster is the unremarkable font used for the title. The rest is a tour de force of quality.

6. The Himalayan (1976)

Another stunner from the vaults of Golden Harvest. The all-action design is right up my street, with all three leads (Angela, Chen Sing and Tan Tao-Liang) having their moment in the spotlight. The aspect of this poster that sets it apart is the background arrangement. No bleached or blended hues, just a striking depiction of soldiers on the march and an impressive Tibetan temple. It's a poster that suggests that the film you're about to watch is an epic.

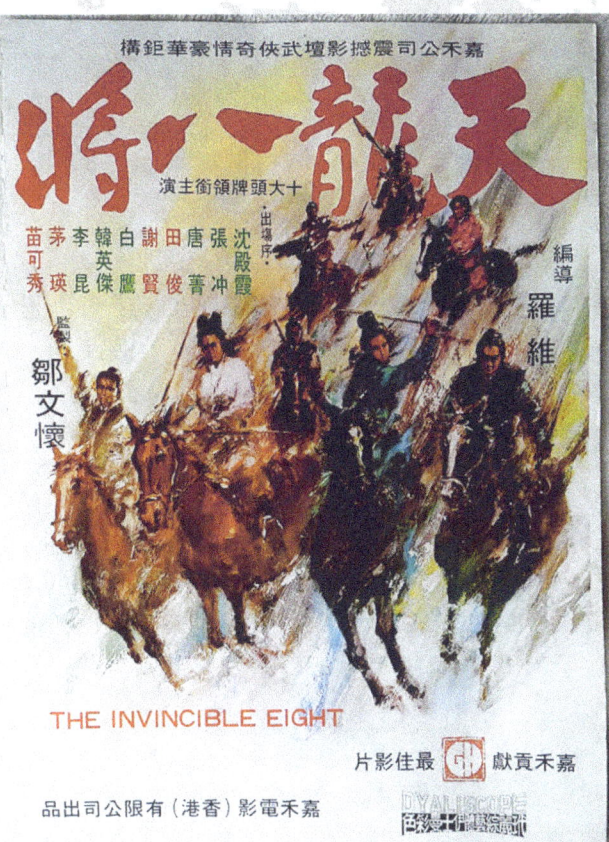

5. The Invincible Eight (1971)

This was one of the first posters I ever acquired, so it holds a special place in my collection. What attracted me to the design back then still attracts me to the design now. That raw flurry of action - half-painted, half-suggested - is absolutely incredible. The way the heads and necks of the horses are clearer than the rest of the body shows real artistic skill. Look at the way each rider is sat. Some holding the reins with two hands, others in a state of preparing a strike. The horses seem to be powering through water, which has enabled the artist to include blues, whites and spray effects. It's an exciting, hi-octane design that I love.

4. Dance of Death (1979)

Question: how many styles can you fit in one poster? Answer: it seems like it's three. For in this poster, we have the cartoony sketches at the bottom of the page, which, to be fair, veer more towards realism than gimpishness. Then we have the more realistic sketches, exemplified by Chia Kai's kicking villain and Angela Mao. Finally, there's the camera film-style sepia movie scenes spread diagonally across half of the background. The best thing about this stunning poster is the picture of Angela. It's an amazing sketch, full of intensity and concentration. Even at the end of the 1970s, her star power was so strong that her image was used to dominate this theatrical poster. It's a stylish, jaw-dropping design.

3. Thunderbolt (1973)

Golden Harvest? Check. Hand-sketched? Check. Horses racing around? Check. Beautiful backgrounds? Check. Exciting action poses? Check. Three Angela Maos? Check. Wait, what? Three?! Who cares – three Angelas for the price of one cannot be a bad thing. This is an absolute belter, near-flawless in its composition and execution. The only thing I'm unsure about is the abrupt jump between colours inside the text. Otherwise, it's a marvel of tonal balance, energy and beauty. I just wish I had the damn thing.

2. Broken Oath (1977)

Narrowly missing the top spot is this stunner from the mid 1970s. I cannot find fault, it's just down to personal preference. Everywhere you look, you're wowed by the intricacies of the design. Angela Mao commands the piece – everything else is built around the powerful image of her holding a staff. The movement of the staff is achieved through motion lines, rather than repetitions of the weapon. The perspective captured by the artist is flawless – it presents our star as authoritative and dynamic. Take a close look around her image. There's almost-spectral figures above her in various stances. They burst from a complicated backdrop of opulent colours, all of which seem to blend seamlessly, despite their diversity. Below her, we have a fight taking place between Michael Chan Wai-Man and Bruce Leung, in front of a row of onlookers. The detail on the faces of the combatants is excellent, yet they are surrounded by scruffy brushstrokes. It denotes a chaos and raw intensity to the scene, captured with great skill. This is a poster that takes a seat in the pantheon of greats.

1. The Angry River (1971)

My first ever poster, but I haven't picked it for that reason. I just can't see past the colour combinations – they're too good. There's posters in this list that are drawn with greater skill, but I can't pretend that every time I look at this poster, my attention isn't arrested completely. Look at Angela Mao's expression – pure, intense, raw strength. This was her coming-of-age as a leading star, and this image captures the power that defined her – in films and on their posters – for the next decade. The bottom half of the poster is no slouch, either, with Kao Yuen and Pai Ying marvellously sketched and coloured. Not an inch of this poster is wasted, yet not an inch is overblown or cluttered. We even have a leaping silhouette and horses! A poster that is epic, yet measured. Powerful, yet subtle. It's simply majestic.

Many thanks to Raymond Farrell and Ka Lok Lam for allowing me to use images from their collections.

FANATICAL DRAGON PRESENTS
5 FINGERS OF DISCS

Greetings friends, your friendly neighbourhood Dragon here once more to shine a light on another few new and upcoming Blu-ray releases well worth your attention and all making a well aimed snake fist grab at your wallets. First off, and announced just in time for our Angela Mao cover issue comes a double bill of two of her most well known and highest rated movies…..

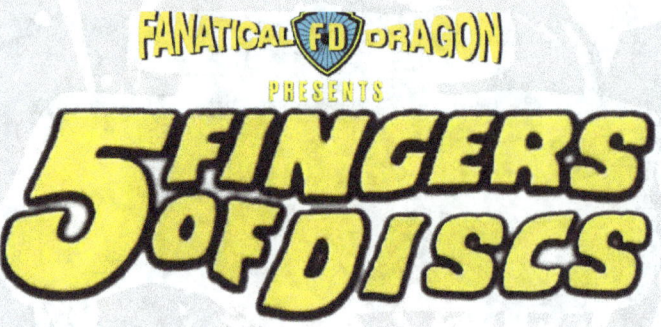

1) Hapkido (1972) / Lady Whirlwind (1972)
Dir - Huang Feng
Eureka Entertainment - Region B
Arrow Video US - Region A
Release Date - August 22nd 2022.

Due for release in late August (22/08/22) Eureka are putting together two absolute gems from Director Huang Feng showcasing Angela Mao's incredible abilities. Hapkido, effectively a loose reimagining of Fist of Fury in which Angela Mao, Carter Wong and Sammo Hung open a Martial Arts school to teach the titular Korean Martial Art Hapkido, fall foul of a rival Japanese school who makes repeated attempts to smash apart the school. A huge fan favourite and a film largely unavailable in the UK since the original (and very rare) Hong Kong Legends DVD release from back in the day.

The second film in the set is arguably Angela Mao's most famous, the incredible Lady Whirlwind aka Deep Thrust a classic tale of revenge that pits Mao up against Shaw Brother's veteran Chang Yi.

Both films in the set are each accompanied by two audio commentary tracks from Frank Djeng, one where he is joined by Eastern Heroes regular contributor Michael Worth, the host of the wonderful Clones Cast Podcast and the man behind the great Pearl River Blu-ray label. A second track where Frank is joined by Martial Artist and Actor Robert 'Bobby' Samuels. That's 4 Commentary tracks in total to dive into across the set! We will also get a brand new video interview with Angela Mao from Frank Djeng (created at the same time as the interview with Angela Mao you'll find within these very pages!)
The set is rounded out with Archival interviews with Angela Mao, Sammo Hung, Yuen Biao and Carter Wong, stills galleries and a selection of TV spots and Trailers.

The Angela Mao set is being released in the UK and will be Region B locked, but fear not

my US friends, in a move becoming more and more familiar as the popularity of Classic Hong Kong movies on Blu-Ray continues to grow, there will be a mirror release of the exact same set in the USA but released by Arrow Video US. The on disc contents will be identical, the only difference will be the cover art.

This will be the second time Eureka and Arrow US have shared a title. The Jimmy Wang Yu classic One Armed Boxer received similar treatment.

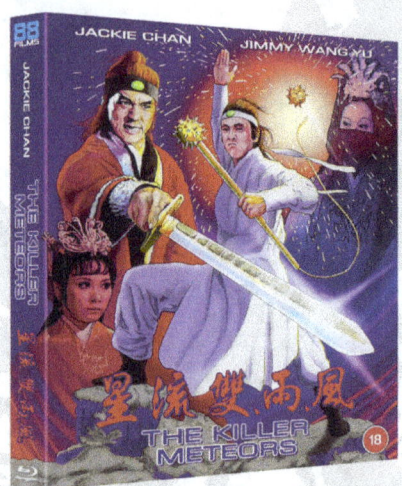

2) The Killer Meteors (1976)
Dir - Lo Wei
88 Films
Region B

Speaking of the late great Jimmy Wang Yu, last month also saw the release of a well regarded and long awaited classic, The Killer Meteors, co-directed by Wang Yu himself along with Lo Wei and also co-starring a young Jackie Chan in a rare villain role. Some pretty great set pieces in this, including an excellent final battle atop a pretty impressive arena built entirely from raised wooden poles.

88 Films effectively kick started this recent craze for loving restorations of HK classics and still now lead the pack in terms of quality of transfers, extras and printed materials bundled along with each release, here we once again get glorious artwork by Kung Fu Bob O'Brien along with a double sided poster and a packed booklet showcasing lobby cards and original posters along with a great article from Matthew Edwards. On disc extra include both Chinese and english dubs sitting alongside a thoroughly entertaining commentary track by Mike Leeder and Arne Venema. The disc is rounded out with the original theatrical trailer.

For those who find this lacking in terms of not enough Jackie Chan (he does just play a supporting role in this, fear not, also released at the same time is……

3) Half a Loaf of Kung Fu (1978)
Dir - Lo Wei
88 Films
Region B

One of the most Marmite of Jackie Chan's early Lo Wei Era movies, either a fan favourite or one of the most hated depending on ones own tastes, this 1978 Kung Fu Parody movie riffs on lots of troupes from Martial Arts movies from both China and Japan (it's not hard to spot Jackie's pretty good Zatoichi impression in the opening credit sequence). It's been one of the movies Chan fans have been requesting most heavily over the past few years and 88 Films have done their usual standout job of restoration, delivering the movie looking and especially sounding better than ever, offering a multitude of Audio choices on the disc.

You can opt for the classic English Dub, Mandarin or two separate Cantonese audio tracks (with differing music cuts).

Extras are rounded out by a commentary track from 88 Films regulars Big Mike Leeder and Arne Venema and the English and HK trailers for the movie.

It comes packaged with the usual glossy O-ring slipcase and double sided poster showcasing gorgeous new art work by Kung Fu Bob O'Brien on the slipcase, cover and poster with the original HK poster art on the flipside of both the cover and the poster.

4) Human Lanterns (1982)
Dir - Sun Chung
88 Films
Region A + B

Another in 88 films spectacular Shaw Brothers numbered series, this entry, No 33 is a pretty damn essential purchase, even for those now trying to collect the whole series. One of the best of the Shaw's horror entires, though arguably much more a Martial Arts movie with horror elements, than a straight horror film (unlike Black Magic, Bewitched, Hex, Seeding of a Ghost or any of the other non Martial Arts Shaw's movies already in the 88 films collection) This fantastic slice of Shaw's history features wonderful performances from Shaw's regulars Lo Lieh and Chen Kuan Tai alongside brief cameos from Venom Mob members Lo Meng and Sun Chien.

The plot revolves around a dispute between two wealthy Kung Fu Masters (played by Chen Kuan Tai and Tony Liu) alongside a revenge scheme being concocted by a unhinged craftsman (played with relish by Lo Lieh)

Gorier than the average Shaw's Kung-Fu movie, but no less packed full with excellent Martial Arts choreography, some great sets and solid practical effects work.

Highly, highly recommended!

Kung Fu Bob once again outdoes himself with a really stunning piece for the Slipcase, inner cover and sketches throughout the booklet, which also showcases an article from Barry Forshaw. Once again we get a foldout reversible poster with Bob's art on one side and the original HK art on the other, this is mirrored on the reversible sleeve.

On disc extras are also an absolute treat, there's a really excellent commentary track courtesy of Kenneth Brorsson and Phil Gillon of the Podcast On Fire Network alongside some absolute interview gems with stars Susan Shaw, Linda Chu and Lau Wing.
Mandarin audio only for this release and the original trailer round out the package.

5) Hero (1997)
Dir Cory Yuen
88 Films
Region B

88's other Shaw Brother's release in May was this, Cory Yuen's Hero, a loose remake of Chang Cheh's seminal Boxer From Shantung, starring Yuen Biao, Takeshi Kaneshiro and Yuen Wah. Whilst nowhere near as beloved as the original (which incidentally you can find in glorious remastered quality on Arrow Video's Shawscope Volume 1 Boxset) the movie has often been overlooked or cast aside completely by many fans. The HD remaster from the original negative breaths new life into the film, and it has aged far better than I expected. The action is maybe a little more reliant on under and over cranking the camera and on liberal use of wire work throughout (as was entirely standard in the 90's era HK action flicks) but overall the movie was way more enjoyable than I had remembered it. This was my first time viewing the film in its original language having only previously seen the English dub (which is also included on the disc) and I found it played even better in it's native Cantonese.

Kung Fu Bob once again delivers on cover art duties, and if you were anticipating me to say it comes with a booklet, poster and reversible sleeve, you would be quite right.
Commentary duties are once again taken care of thanks to HK residents Mike Leeder and Arne Venema giving us their now standard, consistently great mix of facts and laughs. We also get alternate shots included from the Taiwanese version of the movie and English and HK trailers.

This is spine #35 in the 88 Shaw's series (Lau Kar Leung's incredible Martial Club will be #34, but its release has been delayed to the end of July, look out for my full review of it in Issue 6).

6) The Seventh Curse (1986)
Dir - Lam Ngai Kai
88 Films
Region B
Release Date - 4th July 2022

Coming soon from 88 films is a personal favourite of mine, Lam Ngai Kai's absolutely bonkers HK action adventure the Seventh Curse, starring the always wonderful and often overlooked Chin Siu-Ho alongside Maggie Chung and Sibelle Hu and Chow Yun Fat. alongside 'blink and you'll miss them' appearances by scores of other top HK talent including Kara Hui, Chor Yuen, Dick Wei, Wang Lung Wei, Wong Jing, Yasuaki Kurata, Derek Yee and Joyce Godenzi.
The movie is based on writer Ni Kuang's Dr Yuen series of books, and Ni Kuang appears here on camera as Narrator and in a kinda weird, but thoroughly entertaining introduction to the movie.
The franky insane plot revolves around Chin Siu-Ho's Dr Yuen saving a girl from a human sacrifice ritual in Thailand and being poisoned / cursed himself in the process, when the titular seventh Curse hits him he will die despite the best efforts of the girl who saved him (played by the gorgeous Chui Sau-lai) who manages to stave off the curse for one year, Dr Yuen must return to Thailand to face off against the Worm Tribe who cursed him and seek a permanent cure.
Imagine Indiana Jones and the Temple of Doom if Indiana Jones knew Kung Fu and had to battle a demonic monster baby. It's an insanely fun and wild ride.

88 clearly agree that this is something rather special and have pushed out the boat for the release, giving it their 'Deluxe' treatment, so we get a full rigid slipcase with incredible artwork by new 88 Films collaborator Sean Longmore (who has also created jaw droopingly good covers for 88's upcoming release of Righting Wrongs, and their impending 4K release of Dragon's Forever).

They have also produced a bumper 80 page book with articles by Matthew Edwards and Andrew Graves, 6 reproduction Lobby Cards and a poster.
On disc extras are also given the deluxe treatment, we get 3 commentary tracks, two from the master of remaster himself, Frank Djeng, one solo track and one with an as yet unnamed co-host and a third standalone track from Mike Leeder and Arne Venema. We get two cuts of the movie, the longer, uncut HK edition of the film as well as the shorter, export cut. And of particular interest to me, is the addition of a 2 hour long Chin Siu-Ho interview, having been a huge fan of the actor since first discovering him in Shaw Brother's movies like Legend of The Fox and Demon of the Lute and then marvelling at his work in Mr Vampire, Fist of Legend and countless others, i'm really looking forward to such a long form interview with the actor.

The set wasn't available for review as we went to print for this issue, but by the time you read this article, it should be widely available. Worth spending the extra few quid for the deluxe edition in my opinion though if 88 runs true to form, it will more than likely be reissued as a standard release a few months down the line if you're not fussed about the full slipcase, book and lobby cards.

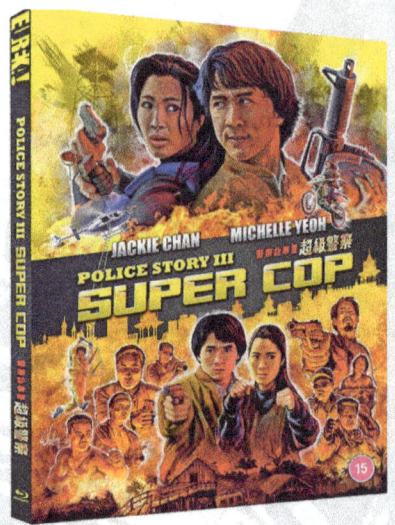

7) Police Story 3 Supercop (1992)
Blu-Ray Release.
Eureka Entertainment - Region B - Release Date - 26th September 2022
88 Films US - Region A - Release Date TBC

Announced just as this article was being put together by Eureka Entertainment comes the news that Police Story 3 aka Supercop will FINALLY be making its debut onto Bluray in the UK in September and just days after that news dropped came an update from 88 Films that they would be putting out Supercop as well, but as a US exclusive. Extras for the Eureka disc have been announced and look pretty damn great. Two different cuts of the movie, the Original 96 minute HK version as well as the shorter 91 min US version (with stars Jackie Chan and Michelle Yeoh Dubbing their own voices in English). Two Commentary tracks on the HK version, from Frank Djeng and from Mike Leeder and Arne Venema along with a mountain of interview footage, including some archival interviews with Chan and Yeoh as well as some new elements provided by the Frederic Ambroisine archives and 50 minutes of NG (outtakes) footage from the movie.

Extras and the exact release date for the 88 Films version of the movie set for a US release are still to be announced.

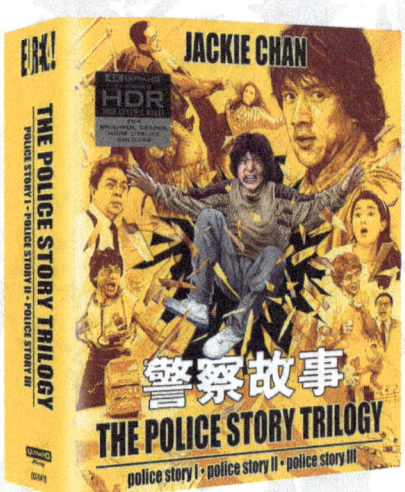

8) Police Story Trilogy (1985/1988/1992)
4K UHD
Eureka Entertainment
Release Date - 26th September 2022

At the same time as announcing their standalone Blu-ray release, Eureka also announced a brand new 4K Police Story Trilogy boxset. With the label taking a leaf from 88's book and hiring the Sharpie Samurai himself, the wonderful King Fu Bob O'Brien to create a stunning cover for the boxset.

Extra are far too numerous to include here without taking a whole extra page to do so, but they include all the extras from the standalone Supercop Blu-ray as well as the extras from Eureka's original Police Story 1+2 Blu-rays.
This will be the first time the movies have been released on UHD anywhere in the world. It looks like a stunning release, as soon as more information is available we'll include it here and I'll be sure to cover it over on my youtube channel too.

If you're reading this and wondering why I've left out the recent batch of great Sammo Hung releases: Knockabout, Dreadnaught, The Shaolin Plot and the re-release of the wonderful Enter the Fat Dragon, fear not! We've been saving them for the Sammo Hung special issue - you can find reviews of all of those titles along with lots more in my 5 Fingers of Discs section when that collectors issue drops soon.

See you all next issue or online, same Kung Fu-Time, same Kung Fu-channel.

Written by Johnny 'The Fanatical Dragon' Burnett

www.youtube.com/thefanaticaldragon

ALTERNATE COVER IMAGE

MEMORABILIA
A SELECTION OF FLYERS & PRESS BOOKS FROM MIKE NESBITT'S PERSONAL COLLECTION

DOLPH LUNDGREN

レッド スコルピオン

ANGELA ON SET WITH BRUCE LEE

THANK YOU'S

We are late out of the blocks with this issue, as we had so much content to add to make this the most comprehensive in-depth look at the life and career of one of the most iconic on screen female fighters

I would like to personally than Frank Djeng and Simon Pritchard for all your hard work in helping out to put this issue together. And a big thanks, to all the other contributors who were interviewed. And of course an extra special thank you to Angela for taking time out, to sit down and be interviewed in depth. Also a big thank you her Son Thomas King for assisting in making this happen

And finally, thank you to all the readers for continuing to support Eastern Heroes without you there is no magazine

Keep the faith

Rick Baker

Rick Baker

Design & Layout
Tim Hollingsworth

www.ingramcontent.com/pod-product-compliance
Lightning Source LLC
Chambersburg PA
CBHW081630100526
44590CB00021B/3674